Croydon's Transport

Through the Ages

Front Cover - Tram in Crown Hill - 3rd May 2001

Croydon's 24 new trams are numbered to follow on from the highest in the former London Transport tram fleet. Here car 2353 descends the steep Crown Hill with the 14th century tower of Croydon Parish Church in the background.

Frontispiece

Part of a map included in a booklet - *The Croydon Railway and its adjacent Scenery,* published in 1840. It can be seen that London had expanded very little to the south of the Thames at that time. The line of the Greenwich Railway, opened between 1836 and 1838 is shown and the London and Croydon Railway, opened in 1839, is in red. This largely followed the alignment of the old Croydon Canal, closed in 1836, but remaining sections of the canal can be seen, marked in blue. The Brighton Railway, then under construction is also shown, in green. This map demonstrates the almost complete lack of population between Croydon and London just over 160 years ago. The scale is approximately one inch to one mile.

Back Cover - Poster about 1910

This attractively coloured poster advertising houses on the Addiscombe Park Estate confirms the importance attached to good public transport facilities in selling properties. It stresses the close proximity to stations and electric trams. Estate Agents continue to use similar words in their advertisements.

£8.75

Contents

Editor - **John Gent**

Published by CNHSS - Croydon Natural History and Scientific Society
96a Brighton Road
South Croydon
Surrey CR2 6AD

ISBN: 0 906047 17 X

Printed by DAP (Sussex) Limited

96 pages   222 illustrations

Copyright - © - CNHSS

October 2001

Introduction

This is the eighth in the series of illustrated books published by the Croydon Natural History and Scientific Society since 1970. The Society was formed in 1870 as the Croydon Microscopical Club. Many of its original members were born in the early nineteenth century before Queen Victoria came to the throne. Some would have known the town when it had the canal and iron railway, before the steam railway came. They would have experienced a completely different way of life and a completely different town from that we know today. This book attempts to record some of the ways in which transport has changed, and changed the town over the years, particularly since the early 1800s. The whole of the present London Borough is covered, although Addington, Coulsdon and Sanderstead were in separate local government areas until the twentieth century. Where pre-decimal currency is referred to, the following conversion table applies;

6 pence = 2½p
1 shilling = 5p
2 shillings = 10p

In preparing this publication it was apparent that each form of transport could justify a separate volume on its own. There are already several much more detailed publications on tramways, railways and the airport but this is intended to give a reasonably complete, albeit brief, survey of all forms of transport in the area. The select bibliography on page 95 lists a number of books containing more information on particular subjects.

Croydon is similar to a gap town. In fact it grew up just to the north of an important gap in the North Downs, which are here at their widest (about seven miles) and reach their highest point (882 feet or about 265 metres above sea level) near Oxted. A number of deep dry valleys through the chalk downs converge south of the town making it an obvious focus for early roads and trackways and, later, railways.

The biggest single factor in Croydon's rapid growth during the nineteenth century and its subsequent importance, is its excellent transport facilities. And the coming of the railway was the catalyst. Thomas Frost gives a description of the town in the 1830s in his *Forty Years' Recollections, Literary and Political*, published in 1880.

"I first saw the light of day in the old and then rather dull town of Croydon, which was however a fair example of the towns of its class, urban centres of agricultural districts, before railways had connected them with the metropolis, or gas lighted their streets....... The long narrow High Street stretched southward, dull rather than quiet, with here a slow grey tilted carrier's cart, and there a Brighton stage-coach, stopping to change horses, with the scarlet coated guard on the back seat, equipped with posthorn and blunderbus......There was little communication with the metropolis and less with the neighbouring towns..... There were persons then living, however, who remembered the time when pack horses were used, a mode of conveyance availed of even during the first quarter of the present (i.e. 19th) century by smugglers who travelled by night, through green lanes and woodland paths, from the coast to obscure nooks on the outskirts of the metropolis...... the application to Parliament for the authorisation of the railway......was the signal for a general chorus of consternation and despair. Everybody, it was said, would go to London to procure the articles which they had hitherto purchased in the town, and the local shopkeepers would be ruined. All the villages below Croydon would send fruit and vegetables to London, and the market gardeners would be ruined. The coaches and the carriers' carts would be driven off the roads, and horses would not be worth an old song". The latter prophesy was of course to some extent realised, and some towns did indeed suffer a decline in trade when served by railway. However rather more, such as Kingston and Uxbridge, suffered from being left behind in the railway building boom.

But some influential residents of Croydon could see the benefits the railway would bring to the town. The *Surrey Standard* of 16th January 1836 reported on a meeting which set up a fund to employ counsel to ensure the proposed Brighton railway should pass through the town and to oppose other projected routes which did not. In the event Croydon soon became an important railway junction, and a convenient place for London workers to live. But in turn it attracted new industries and became a centre of employment in its own right. The main shopping and business area grew to fill the area between the east and west stations, but also spread further north and south along the main road through the town.

But if the railway had the greatest impact, the tram, the bus, and later the motor car have all had a very significant effect. They brought new freedom and opportunities for travel but with adverse environmental effects, as towns have spread their suburbs ever further into the countryside. The development of transport and its effect on the town of Croydon has been replicated in a similar way in many other places. But Croydon is perhaps unique in its number of 'firsts'. It was served by the first public railway in the world. It was the first town in this country to be served by railway and canal. The London and Croydon Railway had the first railway signals, one of only four experiments with atmospheric traction and the first railway flyover in the world. The town had horse and electric trams and trolleybuses, and, also on the roads in 1932 it introduced the first sodium orange street lights and the first light-controlled pedestrian crossing.

Its airport was known throughout the world and was virtually the birthplace of civil aviation. And in the UK at the beginning of the twenty-first century Croydon shares, with Manchester, Sheffield and Birmingham, the benefits of a new modern tram system. This publication introduces the story of these and other developments.

1 Map of Croydon in the 1880s
By the 1880s the railway network south of London was virtually complete, but Croydon was still a separate town with open country on all sides. A comparison of this map with that of 1840 inside the front cover shows that London had expanded tremendously in the intervening years. A link from Selsdon Road station to the Brighton line is shown, but was in fact never built. Construction of the Tattenham Corner branch was still in the future. The scale is approximately one inch to one mile.

Early Roads

The original tracks were made by wild animals. They probably radiated from drinking places and were followed by hunters setting the pattern for later roads. The principal roads in the Croydon area, particularly to the south, show a direct relationship to the valleys and hills, generally, but not always, following the easier route.

The Roman invasion of Britain introduced a network of well-built roads, largely for military purposes but also to help trade. To what extent these followed existing trackways is not known. The principal road through Croydon linked London and Portslade (Brighton) and its course is followed almost exactly by the present A23 road between Brixton and Broad Green. The present road wanders slightly away from a precise straight line because over the years sections of road on the London Clay became impassable after the Romans left and traffic would deviate to take a drier course. This can be seen happening today on footpaths in many of the rural parts of the borough.

South of Broad Green the alignment is in some doubt but Roman finds in and around the town centre suggest it may have followed the present main road and eventually Riddlesdown Road, crossing Riddlesdown to join the present A22 Eastbourne Road near Old Barn Lane.

Another Roman Road, from London to Lewes, ran to the east of Croydon, later forming part of the boundary between Surrey and Kent.

The condition of the roads gradually deteriorated after the Romans left and by the 12th century could best be described as awful. The word "travel" comes from the old Norman-French word "travail", meaning painful effort or exertion! This was (and still can be) very appropriate! Sir Robert More wrote to his father, Sir George, around 1621, that he intended to return with his wife in a coach to Losely, near Guildford, from Sussex. He could not go through Horsham, because it had rained, but he had heard that if he went to East Grinstead, he could find a good road to Godstone, and continue by way of Reigate and Dorking! Later, Daniel Defoe describes how Wealden timber was dragged through Surrey to Deptford, and tree trunks had to be left by the roadside until the next spring if autumn came before the journey was complete.

By the seventeenth century the roads were in a state of neglect. Repairs had been the responsibility of the parish which meant the parishioners who had to contribute six days work on the roads. The better-off could contribute by supplying carts and horses. A familiar sight at this time would have been a footman with an axe walking ahead of a coach to clear the way of trees and shrubs. The incentive for improvements was the Turnpike Act of 1663. This and subsequent measures introduced a scheme for building toll roads and bridges which over time would pay for their construction and maintenance through fees levelled on their users. However the condition of the roads was not the only hazard facing travellers. Highwaymen would rob travellers on the lonely roads well into the nineteenth century.

The horse was still the best and quickest method of travel but coaches were becoming much more common having been introduced from the continent in the sixteenth century. The stage-coach era began in the early seventeenth century and reached its peak in the early nineteenth century. In the early days an average speed of four mph was common. The first regular service from London to Guildford took the whole day, with breakfast and dinner being taken at inns en route. In 1734 the age of speed began, with a reduction in the journey time from London to Newcastle from twelve to nine days! Croydon was a stage-coach posting town where horses were changed at one or other of the principal inns.

2 Green Lane, Norbury about 1906 (above left)
Green Lane is an ancient highway, mentioned in documents as early as the fourteenth century. When this photograph was taken it probably looked much as it had done for centuries, and much as most of Croydon's roads would have looked until the mid-nineteenth century. The road was widened and properly surfaced after the First World War when there was a lot of housing development in the area.

3 Stage-Coach about 1937
Regular stage-coach services disappeared from local roads in the 1880s but enthusiasts used coaches for occasional outings for many years afterwards. Here a coach is travelling along London Road near Thornton Heath Pond, its occupants suitably attired in period costume.

4 Croydon High Street, 1830
In this view the horses of a stage-coach are being changed outside the *Green Dragon* in the High Street. Surrey Street, (then known as Butcher Row) is to the left beyond the inn and the second town hall can be seen beyond that. Opposite the town hall, the inn sign of the *Ship* stood on the pavement outside the hostelry, and attractive houses lined the street. A pack-horse with panniers, commonly used for conveying goods, was being led along the unpaved road.

The first turnpike road in Surrey was opened between Crawley and Reigate in 1696 and the earliest through Croydon was that from Southwark to Ashdown Forest on the way to Eastbourne in 1718. The toll-houses in Croydon were at Norbury just south of Hermitage Bridge, near the *Swan and Sugar Loaf* and at Foxley Hatch (Purley Cross). A new stretch of road was built along the Caterham Valley to avoid the steep climb over Riddlesdown.

The second road to be turnpiked in Croydon was Lower Addiscombe Road/Long Lane near Stroud Green. This took place in 1765 as part of the New Cross Roads Trust which covered an area from Southwark to Lewisham and Farnborough. In 1770 the Limpsfield Trust took over Sanderstead Road from the *Red Deer* to Limpsfield and Edenbridge with toll-houses at Hamsey Green and Botley Hill. The latter still stands. The last local road to be turnpiked ran from Foxley Hatch to Reigate with toll-houses at Lion Green opposite Marlpit Lane and at Merstham.

The Turnpike Trusts were usually set up by private Act of Parliament obtained by a group of local people wishing to improve the trade of their district. The tolls levied were based on the kind of vehicle or type of animal passing along the road. The toll-keeper was often expected to be on duty for 24 hours at a time so his wife would normally have to cover parts of the period. Wages varied from ten shillings to a pound a week. Receipts from the tolls were not high - the busy Foxley Hatch gate taking an average of only £11 a week in 1800.

The Turnpike Trusts were abolished by 1872. The Limpsfield Trust had gone in 1835, the Surrey and Sussex in 1862, the New Cross in 1867, and the Croydon and Reigate in 1872. Maintenance of the roads reverted to the parish and their general condition slowly improved as will be described later.

5 Turnpike Trust Share Certificate

A share certificate for the Croydon and Reigate Turnpike Trust, dated 1808. Most of the subscribers probably made very little profit from their investments as the cost of improving and maintaining the roads was high, and the income generally low.

6 William Inkpen and his Companion, E. Ford, about 1870

Born in 1789, William Inkpen had an office in the High Street from which he ran his stage-coach and saddlery business. For many years he operated stage-coaches between Croydon and London and almost invariably drove one of his teams of horses. He had a strong and not unnatural antipathy towards railways, on which he never once travelled. He was involved with local government for some time, being a member of the Improvement Commissioners and of the Board of Guardians. He was a Director of the Croydon Gas Company from 1847 and Chairman from 1855 to 1858. He died in 1873.

7 Toll-House, Long Lane about 1890
  (below left)
This toll-house, built by the New Cross Roads Trust, stood at the junction of Long Lane (to the right) and Spring Lane (to the left). It was no longer used as a toll-house after the trust ceased operations in 1867, and was demolished in the late 1890s.

8 South End looking north - 1825 (above)
The toll-house and gate of the Surrey and Sussex Turnpike Trust stood between *The Swan and Sugar Loaf*, Selsdon Road and the *Blue Anchor*, which can be seen immediately behind the gate, with Southbridge Lane to the left. On the extreme left is the Bourne stream forming a tributary of the River Wandle, from which the name of the road 'Southbridge', is derived, as there was a bridge over the river nearby.

9 Foxley Hatch Gate looking south about 1815 (below)
This drawing by W. Acock shows the toll-house at Foxley Hatch. It stood on the northern corner of Brighton Road and Godstone Road at what is now known as Purley Cross. There was one gate across Brighton Road and a side gate across what is now Russell Hill Road.

7

10 Pitlake Looking West

Contemporary prints or drawings of the Surrey Iron and the Croydon, Merstham and Godstone railways are very few. This shows the track of the Surrey Iron Railway as it approached Croydon, with the tower of the parish church as a prominent landmark. Contemporary reports suggest that both railways were of double track but it is thought that they may have opened with only one track, and possibly in later days reverted to single track when the traffic was very light. Anyhow, this drawing shows only single track. The rails were flanged, L-shaped and fixed to stone sleepers.

12 Croydon, Merstham and Godstone Railway Notice.

This notice shows that rates of carriage on both lines were comparable. The official opening date for the Croydon, Merstham and Godstone Railway is recorded as 24th July 1805 so this may have been a draft; or the railway may have opened for traffic before the official ceremony - a not uncommon happening that causes problems for later historians seeking accurate information!

11 Surrey Iron Railway Poster

This gives details of the tolls to be paid by users of the railway who, in general, used their own wagons. As the rails were flanged the wagon wheels had a flat base.

SURREY
Iron Railway.

The COMMITTEE of the SURREY IRON RAILWAY COMPANY,

HEREBY, GIVE NOTICE,. That the BASON at *Wandsworth*, and the Railway therefrom up to *Croydon* and *Carshalton*, is now open for the Use of the Public, on Payment of the following Tolls, *viz.*

For all Coals entering into or going out of their Bason at Wandsworth,	*per Chaldron*,	3d.
For all other Goods entering into or going out of their Bason at Wandsworth	*per Ton*,	3d.

For all GOODS carried on the said RAILWAY, as follows, *viz.*

For Dung,	*per Ton, per Mile*,	1d.
For Lime, and all Manures, (except Dung,) Lime-stone, Chalk, Clay, Breeze, Ashes, Sand, Bricks, Stone, Flints, and Fuller's Earth,	*per Ton, per Mile*,	2d.
For Coals,	*per Chald. per Mile*,	3d.
And, For all other Goods,	*per Ton, per Mile*,	3d.

By ORDER of the COMMITTEE,

W. B. LUTTLY,

Wandsworth, June 1, 1804.　　　Clerk of the Company.

BROOKE, PRINTER, No. 35, PATERNOSTER-ROW, LONDON.

CROYDON AND MERSTHAM IRON RAILWAY.

• THE COMMITTEE of the CROYDON and MERSTHAM IRON RAILWAY COMPANY hereby give Notice, That the Railway from Croydon to Merstham is now open for the Use of the Public, on Payment of the following Tolls, viz.

For Dung	1d per Ton per Mile
For Limestone, Chalk, Lime, and all other Manure (except Dung) Clay, Breeze, Ashes, Sand, Bricks, Stone, Flints, and Fullers Earth	2d per Ton per Mile
For Timber, Tin, Copper, Lead, Iron, Charcoal, Coke, Culm, Corn and Seeds, Flour, Malt, and Potatoes	3d per Ton per Mile
For Coals	3d per Chaldron per Mile
And for all other Goods	3d per Ton per Mile

By Order of the Committee,

W. B. LUTTLY,

Wandsworth, 8th January, 1805.　　　Clerk of the Company.

At the end of the eighteenth century, the town of Croydon had a population of some 5,000. It was the principal market town in east Surrey with industries including textile finishing, tanning and brewing. The area around the town produced lime, firestone, fuller's earth and timber and there were market and herb gardens and farms. The River Wandle in its course from Croydon to the River Thames at Wandsworth served the greatest concentration of water powered industry in the London area. Forty factories were recorded along the river in 1805, including 17 concerned with textiles, nine flour mills, five snuff mills, three oil mills, a paper mill, a skinning (leather) mill, a logwood mill, a copper works, an iron works and a brewery. Wandsworth at the mouth of the river was its industrial centre.

In 1799 a group of Wandle valley industrialists proposed a canal up the valley. William Jessop, the celebrated canal engineer, reported that a canal was feasible, but that there was a problem with the water supply. Adverse effects would be suffered by the mill owners and he instead proposed a horse-drawn iron railway. Such railways had been in use in mines and quarries particularly in the north of England since the early seventeenth century. Most had originally used wooden rails but iron had been used more recently. It was therefore decided to proceed with a line from Wandsworth to Croydon, and a branch from Mitcham to Hackbridge.

As a result a Bill was submitted to Parliament in 1801 and the Surrey Iron Railway Act received Royal assent on 21st May 1801. It was significant as the first railway to be authorised by Act of Parliament for general use. Some sections of the line near Wandsworth may have been opened in 1802 but the formal opening took place on 26th July 1803.

England was at war with France from 1793 in what was mainly a naval campaign. There was felt to be a need for a safe inland route between London and the main naval base at Portsmouth to avoid the dangers to sea-going traffic in the English Channel. This was the only practicable route for conveying most bulky traffic and personnel.

At the same time as the scheme for the Surrey Iron Railway was being developed, other interests were proposing The Grand Surrey Canal from Rotherhithe to Camberwell, Mitcham, Croydon, Kingston and Epsom, with the eventual possibility of extending to Southampton and Portsmouth. In the event the scheme developed as a canal from Rotherhithe to Camberwell, with the Croydon Canal as a separate project branching off at Deptford.

William Jessop had foreseen that the Surrey Iron Railway might be the first link in a longer railway and the promoters arranged for a survey of a route from Croydon to Reigate, with Portsmouth again as the ultimate objective. The Croydon, Merstham and Godstone Iron Railway Bill was put before Parliament in 1802 and received Royal Assent on 17th May 1803. The line was formally opened between Croydon and Merstham on 24th July 1805, but the Godstone and Reigate extensions were not built. Both railway companies had difficulty in raising enough capital, and neither seems to have been very profitable. In 1809 the Croydon Canal opened and by about 1810 had laid a railway from its basin at West Croydon to join the other two railways at Pitlake (see plan on page 85). This took away some traffic which previously would have used the Surrey Iron Railway.

With insufficient traffic and small profits the railways allowed their track to deteriorate and the development of steam traction meant that they were soon outdated. The Croydon, Merstham and Godstone line was purchased by the London and Brighton Railway Company in 1838 as it needed two short stretches south of Coulsdon. It is not known precisely when the line closed but parts may have remained open for a few years. The Brighton Railway Board decided to collect the sleeper blocks and rails at Croydon and auctioned them in 1842.

In 1844 the London and South Western Railway and London and Brighton Railway companies developed a scheme to purchase the Surrey Iron Railway and build a new railway on its alignment to link the Brighton line south of Croydon with the South Western line at Earlsfield. The two companies would share the South Western's proposed new terminus at Waterloo. In the event Parliament would not sanction the proposal and the companies disagreed so the scheme failed. In 1846 the Surrey Iron Railway obtained an Act which stated "… the traffic along the said line has ever since the completion thereof been very small, and has of late years been diminishing". It authorised the railway to sell its property and provided for the company to be wound up two years from the date of the Act. Traffic ceased on 31st August 1846.

A few years later, in 1853, a branch line, the Wimbledon and Croydon Railway was authorised, opening in 1855. It had to purchase the trackbed of the Surrey Iron Railway between Mitcham and Waddon Marsh which had already been sold off. In 1997 this branch was itself closed. The alignment has been incorporated into Croydon Tramlink which now uses part of the trackbed of the first public railway in the world designed by William Jessop two centuries ago.

The Croydon Canal

On 27th June 1801, the Croydon Canal Company's Act of Incorporation was passed. This was only five weeks after that for the Surrey Iron Railway. Designed by John Rennie, construction costs were underestimated and it was eight years before the canal opened for trade on 22nd October 1809. The celebrations were described in *The Times* of 27th October.

"On Monday last the navigation of this canal from the Thames to the town of Croydon was opened. The proprietors assembled to celebrate so interesting an event. They met at Sydenham, about five miles from Croydon, and there embarked on one of the company's barges, which was handsomely decorated with flags. At the moment of the barge moving forward an excellent band played 'God Save the King', and a salute of twenty-one guns was fired.

"The proprietor's barge then advanced, followed by a great many other barges loaded, some with coals, others with stone and corn. The zeal and exhilaration of the traders would not let them suffer their barges, loaded as they were, to be destitute of decoration; accordingly they all hoisted flags or streamers and whatever should testify their joy that all their speculations of a profitable traffic were now realised. After passing a wharf erected at Penge Common, by John Scott, Esq., by means of which the towns of Beckenham, Bromley and a considerable part of Kent are accommodated with coals, manure and all other articles of merchandise at a greatly reduced rate of carriage, the gay fleet of barges entered Penge Forest; the canal passes through this forest in a part so elevated that it affords the most extensive prospects comprehending

continued on page 12

13 Chipstead Valley Road, 1823 (above left)
The Croydon, Merstham and Godstone Railway needed rather more substantial engineering works than the Surrey Iron, as it climbed into the North Downs. Several bridges were required to carry roads over the cuttings in the Merstham area, but the only large embankment and overbridge carried the line across the Chipstead Valley. Part of the embankment, now tree-covered, remains alongside the Lion Green car park.

14 The Croydon Canal - 1815 (below left)
This drawing by H. Browne illustrates the attractive and lonely countryside through which the canal passed. It shows a barge on its way southwards approaching the last lock (near the present Honor Oak Park station), before the almost level stretch to Croydon.

15 Old Sydenham Bridge - 1831 (above)
Looking north, the *Greyhound* Inn is just beyond the bridge. Unfortunately no contemporary drawings or prints are known to exist of the canal in Croydon itself.

16 The Old Canal, Anerley about 1904
This coloured postcard view shows the remaining short section of the canal which still exists in Bett's Park, Anerley. It was 'municipalised' with concrete banks many years ago but at the beginning of the twentieth century still looked much as it would have done in earlier days.

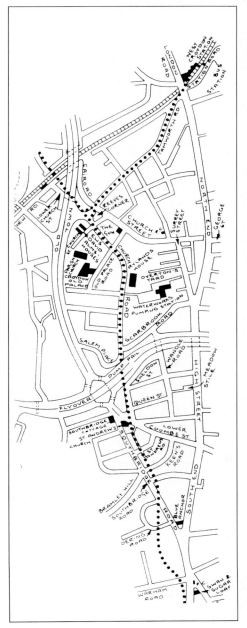

17 Old Sleepers about 1960
Many of the stone sleepers from the Surrey Iron, and Croydon, Merstham & Godstone railways were used for building purposes after the railways closed. The Central Croydon Bowling Club for many years had a pavilion and wall built of sleepers part of which is seen here. The sleepers were removed when the flyover was under construction in the 1960s. Croydon Corporation put them in storage but they were subsequently lost.

18 Railway Alignment in Town Centre
This plan shows the routeing followed by the Surrey Iron and Croydon, Merstham & Godstone railways in the central Croydon area, in relation to the modern road layout.

The Croydon Canal
continued from page 9

Beckenham and several villages and seats, Shooters Hill, Addington Hills, Banstead Downs and numerous other picturesque objects in the counties of Surrey and Kent. The proprietors found their calculations of profit irresistibly interrupted by the rich prospects breaking upon them from time to time by openings among the trees, and as they passed along they were deprived of this grand scenery only by another and no less gratification, that of finding themselves gliding through the deepest recesses of the forest, where nothing met the eye but the elegant windings of the clear and still canal, its borders adorned by a profusion of trees of which the beauty was heightened by the tints of autumn.

"The anxious inhabitants of Croydon met this procession some miles from their town, and hailed it with loud and repeated cheers. When the proprietors neared the basin of Croydon, they saw it surrounded by thousands of persons, assembled to greet with thanks and applause those by whose patriotic perseverance so important a work had been accomplished. It is impossible to describe adequately the scene which presented itself to the feelings which prevailed when the proprietors' barge was entering the basin, at which instant the band was playing 'God Save the King', the guns were firing, the bells of the churches were ringing, and this immense concourse of people were hailing, by universal and hearty and long continuous shouts, the dawn of their commerce and prosperity.

"The proprietors walked from the basin to the *Greyhound*, accompanied by music, and preceded by the workmen, with their tools on their shoulders, enjoying the consciousness of having finished a canal which is allowed to be one of the tightest and best constructed in England".

At the banquet a speech was made in which it was stated that circumstances were favourable for the extension of the Croydon Canal to Portsmouth. The toast was given, "The union of the River Thames and the English Channel through the Croydon Canal".

However the threat from France had receded following the Battle of Trafalgar, technology was improving, and within a few years the steam railway would be competing with and replacing canals so this ambition was never realised.

The Croydon Canal had to rise some 150 feet (about 45 metres) from Deptford to Forest Hill and there were some 26 locks on this section, with two more in the Selhurst area. Wharves were sited at Penge, and later at Forest Hill, Sydenham and Norwood. A military survey of 1811 records the trade principally upwards from the Thames as coals, corn, fir timber, groceries, stone, slate, malt, manure etc, and downwards from Croydon as oak, elm timber, firestone, lime, fuller's earth, flints, flour, seeds etc. The barges did not have living accommodation as they could complete the journey between Croydon and Deptford in one day. They were 60 feet long and nine feet wide. The canal was 34 feet wide, tapering to 24 feet and the towpath was on the eastern bank. Revenue was barely sufficient to cover working expenses and the venture was never really profitable.

Croydon could claim to be the first town in the country to have a railway and a canal. It is very doubtful whether there was sufficient trade to justify this and both the canal and Surrey Iron Railway suffered as a result. However the canal soon became quite a leisure attraction. It opened up large tracts of very pleasant countryside to the north of Croydon and was popular with anglers, skaters in winter, and for outings by boat. This brought some welcome extra income to the company but probably did more for the popular public houses with their tea gardens; the *Dartmouth Arms* at Forest Hill, *The Greyhound* at Sydenham, and the *Jolly Sailor* at Norwood.

By the 1830s there were problems with the canal. The bed leaked in places and the banks fell in at Forest Hill. In 1834 the London and Croydon Railway Company was formed to construct a railway. Joseph Gibb, the engineer to the company, proposed a route from the Greenwich Railway, then under construction, to Croydon, utilising part of the route of the canal. The London and Croydon Railway duly purchased the canal for £40,250 plus one shilling for the profits! The canal closed on 22nd August 1836, together with its railway link to Pitlake.

Local residents can still enjoy angling and sailing at Norwood Lake which was constructed as a reservoir for the canal; but apart from two short sections all that remains is its influence on property boundaries and road layouts in places as illustrated on page 14.

19 Canal Extension Proposal - 1803

20 Canal Barge Sale Poster - 1819

Canal Poem

This poem was included in a booklet entitled
Leaves from the scrapbook of an awkward man
by F.L.Selous - 1844

A DIALOGUE

BETWEEN

THE CROYDON RAILROAD AND THE
CROYDON CANAL.

I.

There 's a lonely dell near Penge's wood,
A wild, umbrageous solitude,
(Hard by that neat, but short-lived Station,*
Whose clerks are enjoying a long vacation ;)
And water lurks in that lonely dell,
Where frogs and efts delight to dwell,
Where weeds lie thick, and the banks are low,
And the muddy stream twines to and fro,
Like a worm that in its slimy course
Man's foot has crushed without remorse.
'Tis the old Canal of Croydon town,
Where a dog *may not* swim, where a dog *cannot* drown.

* Penge Wood station ; relinquished by the Croydon Railway
Company ; soon after the opening of the railway.

II.

And, lo ! from its shallow stagnant bed,
A spirit has raised its wondering head,
And a dirty spirit it was to see,
Just clad, for the sake of decency,
With flags and rushes, and such thin stuff,
And even of those there was barely enough :
It seemed in a fit of unpleasant surprise,
For its mouth was wide open, and so were its
    eyes,
As it stared all around from its filthy flood,
In a pair of those boots that men term " mud."
Now, this I would have you know right well,
Was the spirit of Croydon's old Canal.

III.

Good cause, indeed, had the sprite to stare ;
There was change enough in earth and in air :
New valleys were cut, and bridges were placed,
And pits were filled up, and woods were effaced,
And hills were quite levelled, and swamps were
    drained,—
The devil a thing that he loved, remained ;
Nay, even the air smelt scarce so pure,
As a spirit's nose might well endure :
A little of sulphur, a little of smoke,
Of grease and of oil, of soot and of coke.
'Twas an even bet, if his nose or his eyes
Had greatest reason for such surprise.

IV.

And, behold ! as he gazed, a mightier form,
Like a whirlwind swift, or a gloomy storm,
Came rushing along ! On his ponderous frame
" Sharp, Roberts," was written, (his maker's name,)
His dress was of iron and copper bright,
And he snorted and roared with terrible might.
Oh ! he was a being of fifty horse-power,
Full thirty long miles he moves in the hour ;
And still as he came, with a withering smile,
A pipe of hot steam he smoked all the while.
Oh ! never could words sufficiently tell
The fright of the Croydon old Canal !

V.

Yet he screwed up his courage, and thus he said—
" The devil confound thee, thou spirit ill-bred !
That waketh me thus from the pleasantest sleep,
And maketh my heart in my old bosom leap,
Full twenty long years did quietly glide,
And nothing then troubled my peaceable tide ;
Save perhaps once a week some innocent boat,
With nothing within it, might over me float,
Or some harmless fools might come down by the
    coach,
To angle in vain for gudgeon or roach.
But a visit like this is by no means a joke ;—
And, good Heavens !! what filthy tobacco you
    smoke !"

VI.

Oh ! had you but heard the spirit of steam,
As he roared from his valve,—" Old dotard, you dream
Such folly as yours—or may I be curst !—
So stirs up my fire, my boiler will burst.
What ! know'st thou not *me*, thy country's salvation,
The genius of railroads and civilization,
The spirit of energy, industry, wealth,
Of swiftness, of happiness, cheapness, and health,
That blessings produces and traffic creates,
Though folly opposes, and ignorance hates,
And bigots may fancy they like just as well,
To travel by coach, or the Croydon Canal ? "

VII.

Then spoke the Canal, " Thou worst of my foes,
Dost taunt my misfortunes and brag to my nose :
Base, rascally, railroad, my tears were thy laughter :
Like surgeons, you bought me, *to cut me up* after.*
At present you manage it all your own way,
But perhaps after all the concern might not pay.
I still know some gentlemen, *old* men and *nice*,
Who like half the speed and double the price ;
And the dust, and the rain, and the fees, and esteem
An upset by the coach more than safety by steam ;
Who think *any* profit is made most improperly,
And call all your blessings a shameful monopoly."

* The Croydon Railroad purchased the Croydon Canal, at a very
high price, in order to cut a direct road through and across it.

VIII.

" Thou dozy old god—the water, 'tis plain,
(What little is left) has got on to your brain.
Suppose we did buy you ! pooh !—nonsense and stuff !
Why, every one says we gave more than enough ;
Though we tapped and dissected you, who can be blind,
Like surgeons we cut, for the good of mankind ?
Most dropsical spirit, in vain your reproaches,
We care not a fig for you or the coaches ;
And as for your elderlies—(maniacs at large)—
'Tis a pity they cannot come down by the barge ;
But they might all the way, by the coach with the
    drag on,
Or, better and safer than that, by the waggon."

IX.

Quick flared up old Croydon, " The matter to clinch
I'll appeal on these points to my friend *Mr. Finch,*
That mirror of justice ! I'm sure that he will
Put some sensible, honest, fair clause in your bill ;
Such as, making you furnish your rivals with coke
And water, for nothing. Don't think I'm in joke.
If he had his way, the public should ride
For nothing at all, and be victualled beside.
Though your tax even now to the government mill
Brings more grist than the coaches—he'd burthen
    you still ;
For those who predicted your schemes wouldn't do,
Would look so like fools if their words proved untrue."

* Mr. Finch, the great opposer of Railways in 1840.

X.

Thus answered the Steamer, " Your friend Mr. Finch
Deserves that same law that Yankees call Lynch ;
But to shame and repentance e'en let him live,
For we who are great can afford to forgive :
Each year of success will diminish our foes,
And children will bless what their grandsires oppose ;
Future ages shall witness all prejudice cease,
And nations by railroads united in peace.
But hark ! I am called ; unchecked in my power,
From hence, thirty miles, I fly in the hour ;
Man, stronger than steam, can my presence compel—
I wish you good morning, old Croydon Canal !"

XI.

Away rushed the sprite, to the station again,
Where (from London to Croydon) awaited a train
So awfully long, like the sea-serpent, never
Its head and its tail could be both seen together ;
Then with eyes flashing fire, and nostrils all steam,
He screamed as he flew, such a terrible scream,
That, scared by so loud and infernal a yell,
Right heels-over-head the old water-god fell ;
Deep, deep in the mud, he has buried his head,
No more can he raise it, he dies *in his bed* ;
The magic steam whistle has sounded his knell,
And the spirit is lost of the Croydon Canal.

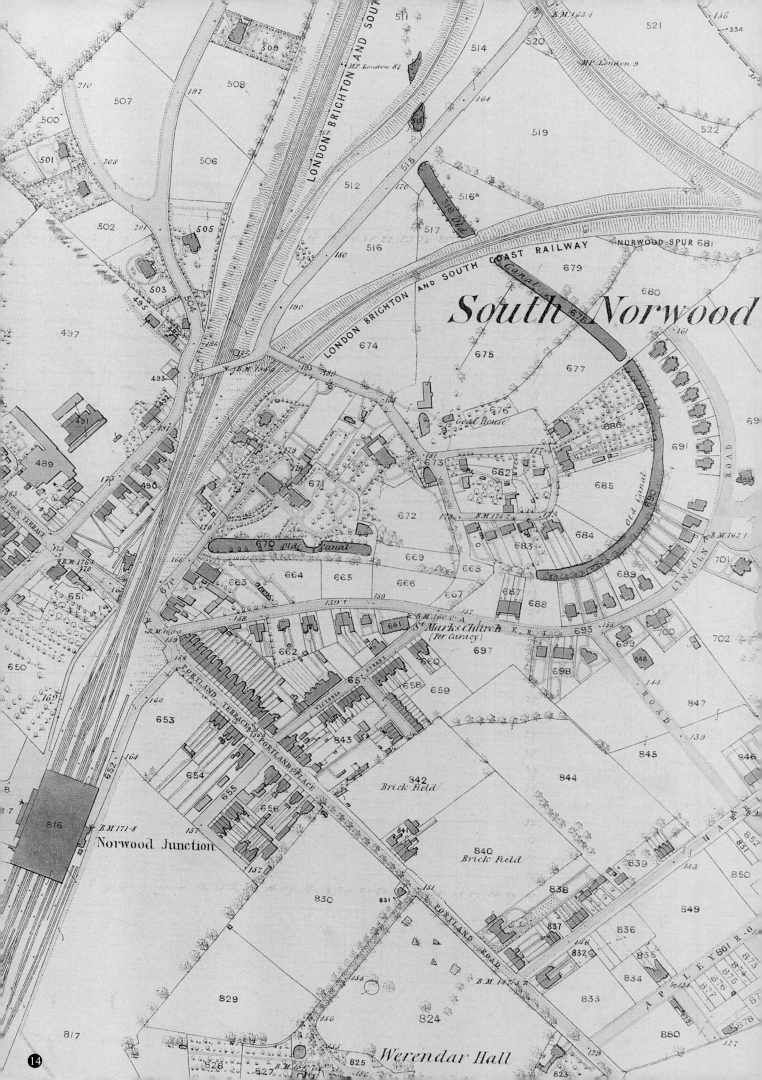

The Railways

The steam engine and its application to railways was a momentous event in the development of our country. Mobility was still very much restricted at the beginning of the nineteenth century but the coming of the railway in a form similar to that we know today changed everything. The 'Railway Mania' started with the opening of the Liverpool and Manchester Railway in 1830. Proposals for new lines abounded. At one time five different routes were proposed for the Brighton Line.

It is very difficult now to appreciate the great impact caused by the coming of the railway. There was opposition from vested interests such as coach proprietors, and, sometimes affected landowners. William Wordsworth and John Ruskin were vocal opponents because of the environmental effects. But Thomas Arnold of Rugby considered the opening of the London and Birmingham line as a notable advance in the march of civilisation and said "I rejoice to see it and to think that feudality is gone for ever. It is so great a blessing to think that one evil is gone for ever". Samuel Smiles, in his Life of George Stephenson, wrote "….the system of British railways, whether considered in point of utility or in respect of the gigantic character and extent of the works involved in their construction, must be regarded as the most magnificent public enterprise yet accomplished in this country; far surpassing all that has been achieved by any government, or by the combined efforts of society in any former age".

The Official Guide to the South Eastern Railway, published in 1858, includes the following comment. "Of the 8,635 miles of railway now constructed in Britain about seventy miles pass through tunnels, and more than fifty miles over viaducts; whilst of railway bridges there have been built some 30,000, or more than all the bridges previously existing in England.

"It is difficult to form an adequate idea of the immense quantity of earth, rock, and clay that has been picked, blasted, shovelled, and wheeled into embankments by English navvies during the last thirty years. On the South Western Railway alone the earth removed amounted to 16,000,000 of cubic yards - a mass of material to form a pyramid 1,000 feet high, with a base of 150,000 square yards. Mr Robert Stephenson has estimated the total amount in all the railways of England as at least 550,000,000 of cubic yards! And what does this represent? 'We are accustomed,' he says, 'to regard St Paul's as a test of height and space; but by the side of the pyramid of earth these works would rear St Paul's would be but as a pigmy to a giant. Imagine a mountain half-a-mile at its base, and soaring into the clouds one mile and a half in height, - that would be the size of the mountain the earthworks would form; while St James' Park, from the Horse Guards to Buckingham Palace,

21 South Norwood - 1868 (left)
This is part of the 25 inches to the mile Ordnance Survey map, reduced to a scale of approximately 19 inches to the mile. When the map was published the Croydon Canal had been closed for just over 30 years but isolated sections remained. Its effect on property boundaries and the alignment of Albert and Lincoln Roads is clear and remains to this day. The way in which the railways, new roads and canal cut through old field boundaries is also apparent. Note that Penge Road, running from centre page left towards top right was originally almost straight, but had to be realigned to veer first left, then right, and left again to take it across the railway at a reasonable angle.

Norwood Junction station had an overall roof but it was destroyed in a gale at about the time the map was printed. The branch line (Norwood Spur) linked Norwood Junction to Beckenham Junction via Birkbeck. A single line remained in use for freight purposes until 1966.

22 Locomotive - 1842 (above)
Number 13 was one of the first batch of Sharp Roberts engines built for the South Eastern Railway in 1841/42. The London & Croydon Railway's engines were similar but in a different livery.

23 Jolly Sailor Station House - 1966 (below)
The original station at South Norwood was known as Jolly Sailor after the (at present) still existing hostelry of that name on the corner of High Street and Portland Road. The station building stood just north-west of Portland Road and is shown on the map opposite with a couple of sidings behind it. The building was demolished in the late 1960s.

CROYDON RAILWAY.

The Public are respectfully informed that on and after FRIDAY, the 1st of MAY, the Trains will start as follow, viz.—

DOWN TRAINS.
FROM TOOLEY STREET.

MORNING.	AFTERNOON.
5 minutes after 8	20 minutes after 4
5 minutes after 9	*20 minutes after 5
5 minutes after 10	* This Train meets the Reigate Coach at Croydon.
5 minutes after 11	
5 minutes after 12	
AFTERNOON.	20 minutes after 6
20 minutes after 2	20 minutes after 8
20 minutes after 3	20 minutes after 9

UP TRAINS.
FROM CROYDON.

MORNING.	AFTERNOON.
5 minutes after 8	20 minutes after 2
5 minutes after 9	20 minutes after 3
*5 minutes after 10	20 minutes after 4
* This Train is in communication with the Reigate Coach.	20 minutes after 5
	20 minutes after 6
	20 minutes after 7
5 minutes after 11	20 minutes after 8
5 minutes after 12	20 minutes after 9

Stopping at the intermediate Stations, viz.,—New Cross; Dartmouth Arms; Sydenham; Anerly, near Westow Hill, Norwood; and Jolly Sailor, near Beulah Spa, and that part of Norwood.

SUNDAYS,

The Trains will start as follow, calling at the intermediate Stations, viz.—

DOWN TRAINS.
FROM TOOLEY STREET.

MORNING.	AFTERNOON.
5 minutes after 8	20 minutes after 4
25 minutes before 5	10 minutes before 5
5 minutes after 9	20 minutes after 5
25 minutes before 10	10 minutes after 6
5 minutes after 10	20 minutes after 6
AFTERNOON.	10 minutes before 7
	20 minutes after 7
10 minutes before 2	10 minutes before 8
20 minutes after 2	20 minutes after 8
10 minutes after 3	10 minutes before 9
20 minutes after 3	20 minutes before 9
10 minutes before 4	

UP TRAINS.
FROM CROYDON.

MORNING.	AFTERNOON.
5 minutes after 8	20 minutes after 4
25 minutes before 9	10 minutes before 5
5 minutes after 9	20 minutes before 5
25 minutes before 10	10 minutes before 6
5 minutes after 10	20 minutes after 6
AFTERNOON.	10 minutes before 7
	20 minutes after 7
10 minutes before 2	10 minutes before 8
20 minutes after 2	20 minutes after 8
10 minutes before 3	10 minutes before 9
20 minutes after 3	20 minutes before 9
10 minutes before 4	

The Servants of the Company are prohibited receiving any Fee or Gratuity.

☞ PARCELS may be BOOKED at ALL the above-named STATIONS.

FARES.

	1st Class.	2nd Class.		1st Class.	2nd Class.
London to New Cross	1s. 0d.	0s. 6d.	London to Jolly Sailor, near Beulah		
— Dartmouth Arms	1 6	1 0	Spa, and that part of Norwood.. 1s. 6d.		1s. 0d
— Sydenham	1 6	1 0	— Croydon	1 9	1 3
— Anerly, near Westow Hill, Norwood	1 6	1 0			

205, Tooley Street,
April 25, 1840.

R. S. YOUNG, SECRETARY.

*** The Passage to and from London and Croydon is performed in about 30 Minutes; and Omnibusses meet every Train at the latter Station.

J. S. WRIGHT, PRINTER, CROYDON.

DAY TICKETS.

In order to afford the Public an opportunity of viewing the

BEAUTIFUL SCENERY

upon this Line, more at leisure than the rapid transit of the trains will now permit, the Directors have given orders that

DAY TICKETS

shall be issued, which will enable the holders, by paying the fare to Croydon and back, *to stop at all or any of the Stations*, and proceed by any other train, in which there may be room, to or from Croydon.

All the trains will stop at the intermediate stations, viz:—

Newcross, Dartmouth Arms, Sydenham, Anerley, near Westow Hill, Norwood, and Jolly Sailor, near Beulah Spa, And that part of Norwood,

By Order of the Board of Directors,

R. S. YOUNG, Secretary.

MARQUEES, &c. ARE ERECTED IN THE WOOD, Close to the Anerley Station, and Parties using the Railway will be permitted to

ANGLE IN THE ADJACENT CANAL, **WHICH ABOUNDS IN FISH.**

---

24 Croydon Railway Timetable - 1840

The London and Croydon Railway ran trains at regular intervals. The Sunday service was more frequent than on weekdays, presumably to attract leisure traffic. There was however a 'church break' between about 10.30 am and just before 2.00 pm when no trains ran. The Victorians were very keen that the Sabbath should be properly observed. The journey time was about 30 minutes; only about two minutes longer than a stopping train in 2001! There are now, however, several more stations and the trains are heavier.

London Bridge station was at this time known as Tooley Street.

25 Advertisement - 1840

Pleasure traffic was encouraged as demonstrated by this advertisement.

27 London and Croydon Railway Offices around 1920 (centre right)

The offices seen here are on the left of the above print. The building was demolished around 1924 and West Croydon station was again rebuilt a few years later with the main entrance in London Road on the bridge.

---

would scarcely afford space for its base. All this mass has been removed by English navvies perhaps the hardest workers in the world". The Victorians had every reason to be proud of their achievements!

The London and Greenwich Railway was the first passenger carrying line south of the metropolis, opening to Deptford in 1836 and on to Greenwich in 1838. The second was the London and Southampton (soon renamed London and South Western) opened in stages from 1838. Parliament had at this time apparently decided there should be only two railway termini south of London and the proposed London and Croydon Railway therefore would run over the Greenwich Railway from London Bridge to Corbett's Lane, paying tolls for the use of the Greenwich tracks.

The London and Brighton Railway would pay tolls to both companies and commence its own line at Selhurst, where it would diverge and run south to Brighton. The South Eastern Railway to Dover would run over the tracks of, and pay tolls to, the Croydon and Greenwich companies and diverge from the Brighton line at Redhill. Ownership of the tracks between Selhurst and Stoats Nest (Coulsdon) would be with the Brighton company, and between Stoats Nest and Redhill with the South Eastern company. These complicated arrangements have led to many problems over the years.

The London and Croydon Railway was formally opened on Saturday 1st June 1839, passengers being carried from the following Wednesday. The cost of construction was around four times the original estimate, great difficulty having been experienced with the cutting between New Cross and Forest Hill. As can be seen from the map inside the front cover, the railway ran through sparsely inhabited open country between New Cross and Croydon. There can have been very little ordinary traffic at intermediate stations and the company soon extolled the beauties of the route, encouraging pleasure traffic.

The London and Brighton Railway opened in 1841, and the South Eastern Railway in 1842. Croydon thus already had two stations, one at each end of the town, and was well-placed for the great growth which would later result. The population of the parish was 12,447 in 1831, 16,712 in 1841, and 20,343 in 1851. The railway seems to have encouraged very little immediate increase. This was no doubt because in common with so many other towns, Croydon was an unhealthy place suffering from poor drainage and lack of a decent water supply until the Local Board of Health was set up in 1851. However after this the population grew much more rapidly, to 30,240 in 1861, 55,652 in 1871 and to 134,037 by 1901! More new railway lines had soon followed. In 1847 the Croydon and Epsom line opened and details are given of the others in the following pages.

Following the Great Exhibition of 1851, the Crystal Palace had to be removed from Hyde Park. The Crystal Palace Company was formed with Samuel Laing as its Chairman to find a new home for the building. He was already chairman of the London, Brighton & South Coast Railway and the Penge estate of Leo Schuster, another director of the railway, was purchased as the site for the Crystal Palace. The expected benefits to the railway company obviously influenced the outcome and the Crystal Palace opened in 1854 with a railway connection. For many years it was a great source of traffic for the railways, and its presence on the Norwood Hills stimulated housing development in the area.

Croydon had very soon become a desirable place for commuters and Professor Jack Simmons wrote in *The Railway in Town and Country 1830 - 1914,* "By 1865 Croydon had grown into the centre of a complicated railway system, running up to five principal London stations and out to Brighton and to junctions with all the chief main lines of south-eastern England....There was no mistaking Croydon's character by that time. It had become a dormitory town. But unlike most dormitories it was also a town in the full sense of the word. It was urban and suburban at once..... Eight stations soon came to lie in the parish of Croydon. By the 1880s there were well over 100 trains to London every week-day; a more lavish service than that enjoyed by any other place over a distance of ten miles. It had become, to a degree unmatched among old market towns, a residence chosen by commuters".

The remaining countryside between Croydon and London was virtually covered in houses by the 1920s. The districts along the original line to London Bridge in general developed sooner than those on the 1862 line between Balham and Selhurst. This was no doubt partly due to the presence of the Crystal Palace, but most commercial activity at that time took place in the City. The West End developed much later as a place in which to work.

The later growth of Croydon in the 1960s as a major office and employment centre, and its present commercial importance are a direct result of the excellent railway links to the town that came about through the efforts of the Victorian railway builders over a hundred years earlier.

Railway Terminus Croydon

26 Croydon Railway Terminus - about 1840
(above right)
This print shows the original station building at West Croydon. Early one Wednesday morning in September 1846 it caught fire and the *Illustrated London News* reported that "Fortunately the servants of the Company and police succeeded in saving the stock. The usual intelligence was, without delay, sent to the engine stations of the town, and forthwith the barrack and parish engines reached the scene of the fire. By that period the whole of the old locomotive depot was enveloped in flame and upwards of a dozen first and second class carriages were in flames. When the London engines arrived for some time the greatest difficulty was experienced in obtaining a supply of water; meanwhile the flames progressed with such rapidity that before four o'clock both the stations (the present atmospheric, and the old locomotive) presented an immense body of flame".
The original station building was destroyed and had to be rebuilt.

28 Plan of Croydon Station - 1839

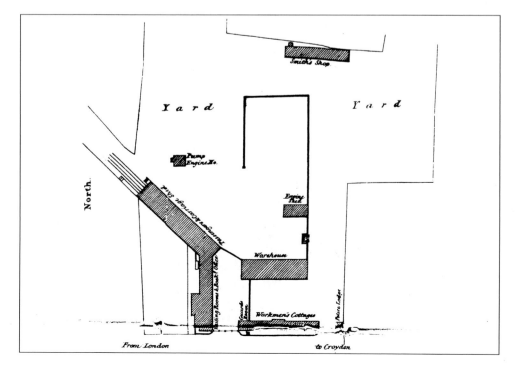

29 The London and Croydon Railway at New Cross - 1838 (above)

Looking north, the arches of the viaduct of the Greenwich Railway run across in the distance from left to right, with market gardens and fields covering most of the land between it and New Cross station. The road bridge and the steep sides of the cutting are in the foreground. This print predates the opening of the railway and it will be noted that the train, presumably on test, is running on the right, rather than on the left as soon became common practice. The Greenwich Railway ran on the right until the Croydon line opened in 1839.

30 Building the Brighton Railway, Croydon, 1840 (below)

The new bridge carrying Coombe Road is in the centre, with Park Hill, and what is now Coombe Cliff on the left. Railway construction in the early days was highly labour-intensive using many navvies. The word navvy comes from navigator. It was the name given to the canal-builders of the eighteenth century and was inherited by the railway builders. They lodged in villages or towns, or in temporary camps and could cause terror in the neighbourhood. Attempts to give them religious and other instruction were sometimes appreciated - often not. A lay reader, Thomas Jenour, worked among the 400 men employed on the Croydon and Epsom Railway. He started a school on winter evenings and taught reading, writing and arithmetic. Not more than twenty of the men could read at first but in two months he had taught most to read a little. He also wrote letters for them and acted as a sort of social restraint against their possible excesses of drinking and womanising.

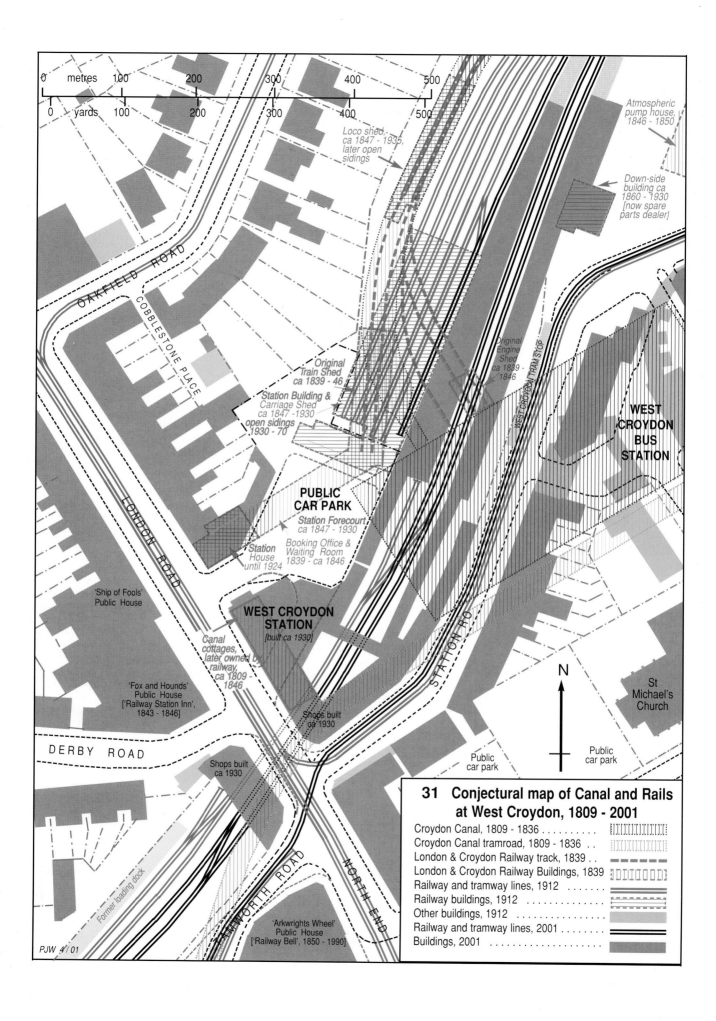

31 Conjectural map of Canal and Rails at West Croydon, 1809 - 2001

Croydon Canal, 1809 - 1836	
Croydon Canal tramroad, 1809 - 1836	
London & Croydon Railway track, 1839	
London & Croydon Railway Buildings, 1839	
Railway and tramway lines, 1912	
Railway buildings, 1912	
Other buildings, 1912	
Railway and tramway lines, 2001	
Buildings, 2001	

Atmospheric pump house, 1846 - 1850

Down-side building ca 1860 - 1930 [now spare parts dealer]

Loco shed, ca 1847 - 1935, later open sidings

WEST CROYDON BUS STATION

Original Engine Shed ca 1839 - 1846

Original Train Shed ca 1839 - 46

Station Building & Carriage Shed ca 1847 - 1930 open sidings 1930 - 70

WEST CROYDON TRAM STOP

PUBLIC CAR PARK

Station Forecourt ca 1847 - 1930

Booking Office & Waiting Room 1839 - ca 1846

Station House until 1924

St Michael's Church

'Ship of Fools' Public House

WEST CROYDON STATION [built ca 1930]

Canal cottages, later owned by railway, ca 1809 - 1846

'Fox and Hounds' Public House ['Railway Station Inn', 1843 - 1846]

Shops built ca 1930

N

Public car park

Public car park

DERBY ROAD

Shops built ca 1930

Former loading dock

'Arkwrights Wheel' Public House ['Railway Bell', 1850 - 1990]

OAKFIELD ROAD

COBBLESTONE PLACE

LONDON ROAD

STATION RD

NORTH END

PJW 4/01

Railway station names

Addiscombe
Croydon (Addiscombe Road) 1864 - 1925
Croydon (Addiscombe) 1925 - 1926
Addiscombe 1926 - 1997

Bingham Road
Bingham Road Halt 1906 - 1915
Bingham Road 1935 - 1983
[Tramlink: Addiscombe 2000 -]

Central Croydon 1868 - 1871, 1886 - 1890

Coombe Road:
Coombe Lane 1885 - 1915
Coombe Road 1935 - 1983

Coulsdon North:
Stoats Nest 1899 - 1911
Coulsdon & Smitham Downs 1911 - 1923
Coulsdon West 1923
Coulsdon North 1923 - 1983

Coulsdon South:
Coulsdon 1889 - 1896
Coulsdon & Cane Hill 1896 - 1923
Coulsdon East 1923
Coulsdon South 1923 -

East Croydon:
opened 1841 as Croydon
New Croydon added 1862 - 1909

Jolly Sailor 1839 - 1846

Kenley
opened 1856 as Coulsdon
Kenley 1856 -

Norbury 1878 -

Norwood Junction:
Jolly Sailor 1846 - 1859
Norwood Junction and South Norwood 1859 - 1910
Norwood Junction 1910 -

Purley:
Godstone Road 1841 - 1847
Caterham Junction 1856 - 1888
Purley 1888 -

Purley Oaks 1899 -

Reedham 1904 -

Riddlesdown 1927 -

Sanderstead 1884 -

Selhurst 1865 -

Selsdon:
Selsdon Road 1885 - 1935
Selsdon 1935 -

Smitham 1904 -

South Croydon 1865 -

Spencer Road Halt 1906 - 1915

Stoats Nest 1841 - 1856

Thornton Heath 1862 -
originally Colliers Water Lane

Waddon 1863 -

Waddon Marsh 1930 - 1997
[Tramlink 2000 -]

West Croydon:
Croydon 1839 - 1851
West Croydon 1851 -

Whyteleafe 1900 -

Woodmansterne 1932 -

Woodside
Woodside & South Norwood
1871 - 1955
Woodside 1955 - 1997
[Tramlink 2000 -]

The Atmospheric Railway

This was an early attempt to power a railway from a central source instead of using individual steam engines. A tube, about a foot in diameter, was laid between the rails. The leading vehicle of each train had an arm attached to it, projecting downwards from its underside. This arm passed through a continuous slot in the top of the tube and was connected to a piston which fitted closely into the tube. A leather flap was fitted over the slot, thus closing it, but this flap could lift in front of the arm which connected piston and train, and likewise close behind it. Thus, as a train moved along the track, the pipe remained sealed.

Power was generated by stationary steam engines situated about every three miles along the line. These drove air suction pumps which exhausted the air from the tube ahead of the train, thus creating a partial vacuum in front of the train piston. The pressure of the atmosphere working on the rear of the piston then forced the train along. Only four such lines were ever built although many were projected. One was in Croydon, another in Dublin, one on part of the South Devon Railway, and a fourth in Paris.

In the early 1840s the London and Croydon Railway was experiencing congestion with growing traffic, and South Eastern and Brighton trains sharing its tracks. It therefore decided to lay a third line and use atmospheric traction. The line opened between Forest Hill and Croydon on 14th January 1846, with stationary engines at Forest Hill, Norwood and Croydon. The line was extended to New Cross in February 1847, but the Croydon and Brighton companies had by then merged to form the London, Brighton and South Coast Railway. The many problems with the system caused its abandonment on 3rd May 1847.

Had the system been introduced later in the century as technology improved it might well have been successful, but its unreliability led to its abandonment on all the lines within a few years.

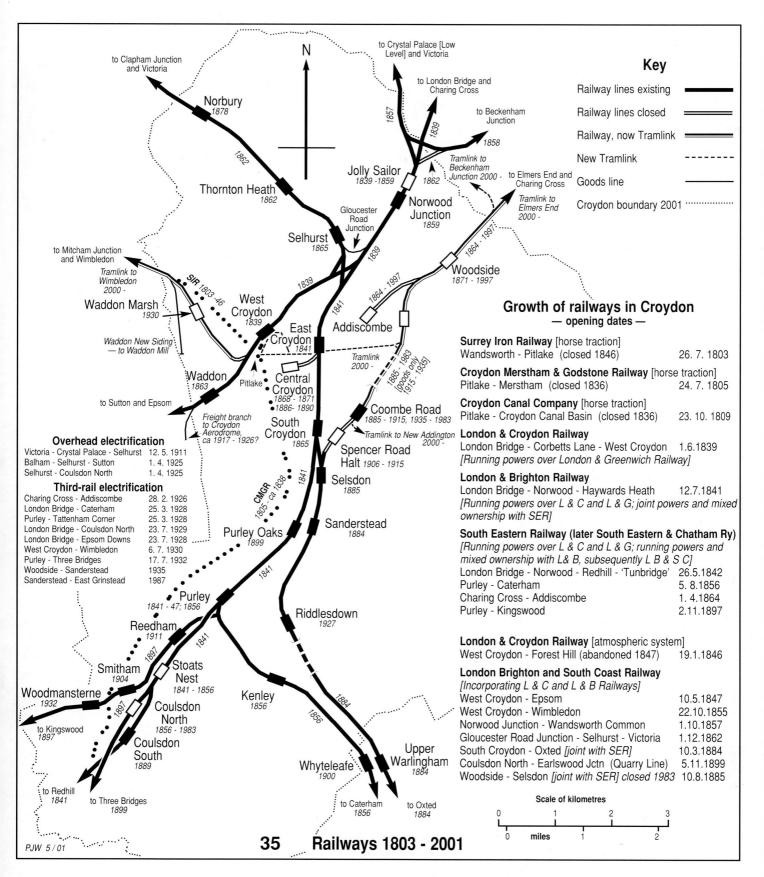

Key

Railway lines existing	▬▬▬▬
Railway lines closed	═════
Railway, now Tramlink	━━━━━
New Tramlink	------
Goods line	────
Croydon boundary 2001	········

N

to Clapham Junction and Victoria

Norbury *1878*

1862

Thornton Heath *1862*

to Crystal Palace [Low Level] and Victoria

to London Bridge and Charing Cross

to Beckenham Junction

1857

1839

1858

Jolly Sailor *1839 -1859*

1862

Tramlink to Beckenham Junction 2000 -

to Elmers End and Charing Cross

Tramlink to Elmers End 2000 -

Gloucester Road Junction

Norwood Junction *1859*

Selhurst *1865*

1864 - 1997

Woodside *1871 - 1997*

to Mitcham Junction and Wimbledon

Tramlink to Wimbledon 2000 -

SIR 1803 -46

Waddon Marsh *1930*

West Croydon *1839*

1839

1841

1864 -1997

Addiscombe

Waddon New Siding — to Waddon Mill

East Croydon *1841*

Tramlink 2000 -

1885 - 1983 [goods only 1915 -1935]

Waddon *1863*

Pitlake

Central Croydon *1868 - 1871* *1886 - 1890*

Coombe Road *1885 - 1915, 1935 -1983*

to Sutton and Epsom

Freight branch to Croydon Aerodrome, ca 1917 - 1926?

South Croydon *1865*

Tramlink to New Addington 2000 -

Spencer Road Halt *1906 - 1915*

Growth of railways in Croydon
— opening dates —

Surrey Iron Railway [horse traction]
Wandsworth - Pitlake (closed 1846)   26. 7. 1803

Croydon Merstham & Godstone Railway [horse traction]
Pitlake - Merstham (closed 1836)   24. 7. 1805

Croydon Canal Company [horse traction]
Pitlake - Croydon Canal Basin (closed 1836)   23. 10. 1809

London & Croydon Railway
London Bridge - Corbetts Lane - West Croydon   1.6.1839
[Running powers over London & Greenwich Railway]

London & Brighton Railway
London Bridge - Norwood - Haywards Heath   12.7.1841
[Running powers over L & C and L & G; joint powers and mixed ownership with SER]

South Eastern Railway (later South Eastern & Chatham Ry)
[Running powers over L & C and L & G; running powers and mixed ownership with L & B, subsequently L B & S C]
London Bridge - Norwood - Redhill - 'Tunbridge'   26.5.1842
Purley - Caterham   5. 8.1856
Charing Cross - Addiscombe   1. 4.1864
Purley - Kingswood   2.11.1897

London & Croydon Railway [atmospheric system]
West Croydon - Forest Hill (abandoned 1847)   19.1.1846

London Brighton and South Coast Railway
[Incorporating L & C and L & B Railways]
West Croydon - Epsom   10.5.1847
West Croydon - Wimbledon   22.10.1855
Norwood Junction - Wandsworth Common   1.10.1857
Gloucester Road Junction - Selhurst - Victoria   1.12.1862
South Croydon - Oxted [joint with SER]   10.3.1884
Coulsdon North - Earlswood Jctn (Quarry Line)   5.11.1899
Woodside - Selsdon [joint with SER] closed 1983   10.8.1885

Overhead electrification
Victoria - Crystal Palace - Selhurst   12. 5. 1911
Balham - Selhurst - Sutton   1. 4. 1925
Selhurst - Coulsdon North   1. 4. 1925

Third-rail electrification
Charing Cross - Addiscombe   28. 2. 1926
London Bridge - Caterham   25. 3. 1928
Purley - Tattenham Corner   25. 3. 1928
London Bridge - Coulsdon North   23. 7. 1929
London Bridge - Epsom Downs   23. 7. 1928
West Croydon - Wimbledon   6. 7. 1930
Purley - Three Bridges   17. 7. 1932
Woodside - Sanderstead   1935
Sanderstead - East Grinstead   1987

Selsdon *1885*

1841

CMGR *1805 - ca 1838*

Sanderstead *1884*

Purley Oaks *1899*

Purley *1841 - 47; 1856*

Reedham *1911*

1841

Riddlesdown *1927*

Smitham *1904*

1897

Stoats Nest *1841 - 1856*

Kenley *1856*

Woodmansterne *1932*

1897

Coulsdon North *1856 - 1983*

to Kingswood *1897*

Coulsdon South *1889*

1856

1884

Whyteleafe *1900*

Upper Warlingham *1884*

to Redhill *1841*

to Three Bridges *1899*

to Caterham *1856*

to Oxted *1884*

Scale of kilometres

0   1   2   3

0   miles   1   2

35   Railways 1803 - 2001

PJW 5 / 01

32 Piston Carriage and Driver on Croydon Atmospheric Line (above left)

33 Atmospheric Railway Tube (centre left)
This was dug up during building work at West Croydon in the 1930s. It is thought many tubes remain for drainage purposes under the existing tracks between New Cross Gate and Croydon.

34 Atmospheric Railway Flyover (below left)
Conventional junctions were not possible because of the tube. To bring the atmospheric line from the south side of the Brighton line to West Croydon it was necessary to carry it across on this timber viaduct at Selhurst. The first railway flyover in the world, its replacement still carries trains from Norwood Junction to West Croydon today.

36, 37, 38, 39 and 40 Central Croydon Station - 1890

The South Eastern and Brighton companies had an uneasy relationship to say the least. The South Eastern's Mid-Kent Railway was originally intended to reach the Fairfield area, but in the event (1864) only reached Addiscombe Road (neither mid nor Kent). The Brighton company built a very short branch to terminate alongside the newly built Katharine Street. The new station was named Central Croydon but was never very successful, opening in 1868, closing in 1871, reopening in 1888, and closing finally in 1890. It was used mainly by through train services of the Great Eastern from Liverpool Street and London and North Western from Willesden Junction. After closure the station site was used for the new town hall, the adjacent gardens being laid out in the cutting. Sidings and engineering works remained in use on Fairfield until the 1930s.

41 Ordnance Survey Map - 1868

Part of the 25 inches to the mile map showing the Central Croydon branch and the layout of East Croydon station before it was rebuilt in 1894. At one time the Brighton and South Eastern companies reached agreement to charge the same fares between East Croydon and London. The Brighton company then opened new platforms, called that part of the station New Croydon, and charged cheaper fares from there!

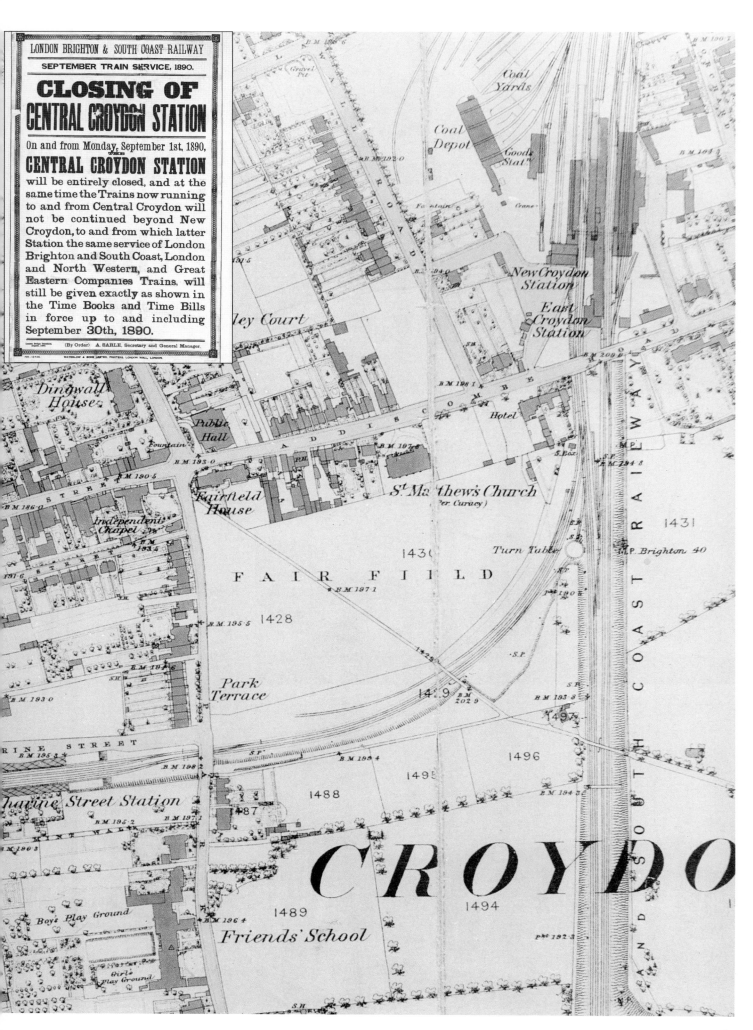

LONDON BRIGHTON & SOUTH COAST RAILWAY

SEPTEMBER TRAIN SERVICE, 1890.

CLOSING OF
CENTRAL CROYDON STATION

On and from Monday, September 1st, 1890,
THE
CENTRAL CROYDON STATION
will be entirely closed, and at the
same time the Trains now running
to and from Central Croydon will
not be continued beyond New
Croydon, to and from which latter
Station the same service of London
Brighton and South Coast, London
and North Western, and Great
Eastern Companies Trains, will
still be given exactly as shown in
the Time Books and Time Bills
in force up to and including
September 30th, 1890.

(By Order) A. SARLE, Secretary and General Manager.

WATERLOW & SONS LIMITED, PRINTERS, LONDON WALL, LONDON.

London, Brighton and South Coast Railway.

NOTICE.

On and after the 1st October next

THE NAME OF

CATERHAM JUNCTION

STATION

WILL BE

ALTERED TO

PURLEY.

(By Order)   A. SARLE, Secretary & General Manager.

JULY 2nd, 1888.

Waterlow and Sons Limited, Printers, London Wall, London.

**42 Caterham Junction Station 1880
and 43 renaming poster** (above)

The Brighton Railway opened a station amongst the lonely downs in 1841. Called Godstone Road it had closed by 1847 but reopened as Caterham Junction in 1856 when the Caterham Railway Company opened its line along the valley. The South Eastern company soon took the branch over but passengers endured some years of hassle as that company and the Brighton company, (who owned the junction station) generally made life difficult for them.

44 Kenley Station about 1908 (left)

Opened as Coulsdon in 1856, the station was soon renamed. The attractive building dates from the opening of the line and remains largely unaltered although now in private use.

45 Addiscombe Station about 1899
(left)

The terminus of the inappropriately named Mid-Kent Railway was opened in 1864. It was intended to tap the lucrative traffic from a growing part of Croydon. Originally there was a turntable in what later became the station forecourt. The station was rebuilt in 1900 and closed on 31st May 1997 when work started on the Tramlink project. See illustration 80 on page 38 for photograph of the later station which was demolished in 2001.

46 Poster - 1892 (above right)

Vandalism and criminal activity on public transport obviously is not just a recent development.

47 Sanderstead Station Looking North, 1884

(above right)

In 1865 the Surrey and Sussex Junction Railway obtained its Act for a line (to be worked by the Brighton company) from South Croydon to Tunbridge Wells. At that time the local lines were being extended from New/East Croydon to a new terminus at South Croydon. Following rows with the South Eastern Company which considered the proposed new line an incursion into its area, work on the line stopped after several bridges and embankments had been built.

After about 15 years a line was built following almost the same route. The Croydon, Oxted and East Grinstead Railway was a joint Brighton and South Eastern venture and opened on 10th March 1884.

In the late 1920s the Southern Heights Light Railway was proposed to link Sanderstead and Orpington via Tatsfield. It was shown on Southern Railway maps but the proposal was dropped in the 1930s.

48 Train at Selsdon Road about 1890

(centre right)

While the Croydon, Oxted and East Grinstead Railway was under construction the Brighton and South Eastern companies promoted the Woodside and South Croydon Railway to link the Mid-Kent line and the Oxted line at Selsdon Road. This opened as a joint venture on 10th August 1885. For some time it was worked by each company for alternate years.

In this photograph one of Stroudley's famous 'Terrier' locomotives (of which ten have been preserved), is standing by the north signal box with a train of antiquated, (although quite common at that time) four-wheel coaches. Note the oil-lamps on the carriage roofs which provided limited illumination at night.

49 Spencer Road Halt - 1931 (right)

Opened in 1906 this halt had a short life, closing with the passenger service on the line in 1915. The tracks were still used by occasional trains such as this Hastings excursion on 13th September 1931. The line was electrified and reopened on 30th September 1935, but the halt was never revived.

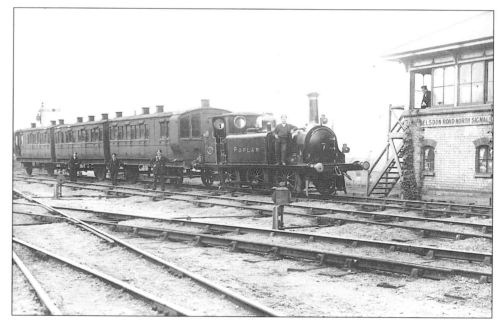

50 Building the Tattenham Corner Line - about 1898 (left)
This was the last new railway line to be built in the Croydon area. The South Eastern opened the line as far as Kingswood on 2nd November 1897, to Tadworth on 1st July 1900, and to Tattenham Corner on 4th June 1901. The precise location of this photograph is not recorded but it does illustrate the type of machinery in use. Building railways at the end of the nineteenth century was not nearly as labour-intensive as in the early years.

51 Widening the Railway at Norbury - 7th June 1903 (below)
The first route between Croydon and Victoria was via the West End of London and Crystal Palace Railway, opened in 1857. On 1st December 1862 the direct line from Selhurst to Balham was opened. By the end of the nineteenth century the Brighton company decided it needed widening to accommodate the growing traffic. This was done and the quadrupled tracks opened on 6th July 1903, a month after this photograph was taken.

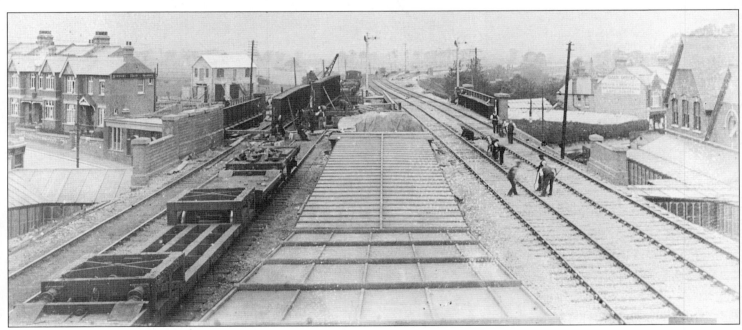

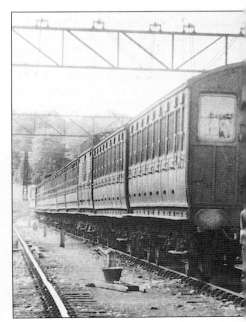

52 Local train about 1910 (below left)
Here a local train is travelling north between Thornton Heath and Norbury before housing development had joined Croydon and London.

53 LNWR Train at East Croydon about 1920 (right)
The London and North Western Railway ran direct passenger trains to Croydon for many years. Here one of Webb's LNWR 2-4-2 tank locomotives stands at East Croydon with a train for Willesden Junction. A new service from Brighton /Gatwick via Croydon to Rugby on the North Western main line was introduced in 1997.

54 Waddon Station - 1934 (centre right)
The London and Croydon Railway promoted an extension as the Croydon and Epsom Railway which opened in 1847. It was not until 1863 that a station was opened at Waddon. The original station, seen here with homeward bound commuters, was replaced around 1937.

55 Electric Trains - 10th July 1928 (below)
In the early years of the twentieth century, the London, Brighton and South Coast Railway experienced severe competition from the new electric trams in south London. On 1st December 1909 electric traction was introduced on the South London Line between London Bridge and Victoria via Brixton and Peckham. Traffic doubled within a few months and the company then decided to electrify the Victoria to Crystal Palace line which was inaugurated on 12th May 1911. In association with this the electrification was extended to Selhurst where a new depot was built.

This early electrification used 6,700 volts AC on the overhead wire principle. The lines to Coulsdon North and Sutton were electrified from 1st April 1925. Meanwhile the railways nationally had been grouped into four large companies in 1923. The newly-formed Southern Railway decided to use the third-rail 600 volts DC system that was already in use on some South Western lines. Here an overhead electric train on the left was alongside one of the third-rail trains on the right at Coulsdon North. The AC overhead system was finally abandoned on 22nd September 1929.

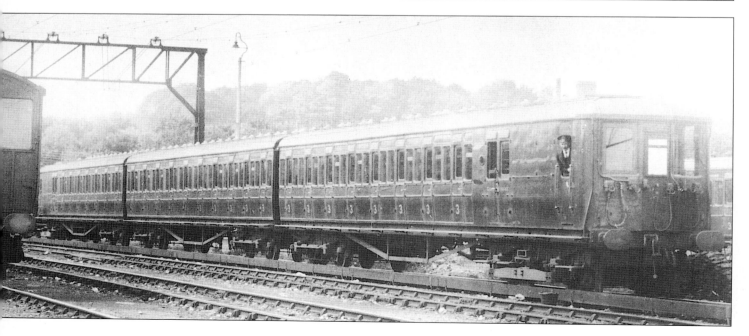

The Railwaymen

The railways brought employment to many thousands of people. At one time more people were employed on Britain's railways than in almost any other industry and almost every trade was represented. Hours were long, conditions hard and the work could be dangerous but a proud tradition of service grew up and in many families it became common for successive generations to follow each other into the industry. There was a strong military influence as strict adherence to regulations was needed to ensure safety. The railways were 'Common Carriers' until the mid-twentieth century and had to carry virtually any goods, hence the large number of sidings and goods yards on the network.

W.G. (Bill) Tharby remembers
Bill Tharby worked for the railways from around 1910 until 1961. In 1969 he wrote some of his recollections and the following is an extract. Bill died in 1979.

"I worked at Norbury station from 1914 to 1916. It was too built up for my liking, although the view from the main entrance to the station was rural, with first a wooden fence, then a golf course, and beyond that trees. It was possible to go for a country walk by taking a lane across the golf course then turning left along the ridge where the trees grew, thence keeping forward in a northerly direction to The Rookery and out on to Streatham Common. On the west side of the road where the trams ran the roads did not go back very far, and fields utilised by market gardeners were soon reached. A muddy lane led to Mitcham Common. I worked alternate Sundays from the first to last train, a period of 17 hours, the only way to get the other Sundays off duty. I used to cycle from Coulsdon and carry breakfast, mid-day meal, tea and supper in a large wicker basket. Supper usually disappeared earlier in the day and between trains I often patronised a nearby coffee stall, where saveloys and other delicacies were obtainable.......

".......a short distance north of Hermitage Bridge is the *William the Fourth* public house. In those days, being in the London County Council area, it remained open later than the Croydon pubs, and soaks used to travel up to Norbury by tram to enjoy extra drinking time. By the time it closed the trams had ceased to run, and those 'sons of suction' returned by train. By that time they were often far gone and we were treated to 'there's an old mill by the stream, Nellie Dean' more or less in tune.

When on late duty I was allowed to travel to Coulsdon on the 12.38 am train, the last down. One Coulsdon engine driver, Jimmy Shaw, used to let me travel on the footplate. He would sometimes say 'catch hold of the regulator handle, lad', which was a great thrill. It was a rough ride on the footplate of the little Stroudley tank engine which had his name painted in the cab. Jimmy, who lies in the churchyard at Woodmansterne, was a very strong man. One day a porter standing on the ground was talking to him, and suddenly he leaned down and grabbed the porter in one hand and hauled him up on to the footplate saying 'come up here lad, where I can hear what you are saying'.

"Like Coulsdon and Smitham Downs, Norbury had a small telegraph office abutting on to the booking office and we had many Post Office telegrams to transmit by single needle telegraph".

In 1916 Bill was transferred to Honor Oak Park and then joined The Royal Navy. In January 1919 he was demobilised.

"My parents were now living in Croydon, and I had written to the L.B. & S.C.R. asking to be stationed where I could live at home. I was instructed to report to the Station Superintendent at East Croydon. This station, together with the London termini, plus Brighton, Eastbourne and Portsmouth, had top-hatted Stationmasters who were called Station Superintendents. The toppers and titles outside London disappeared with the grouping of 1923..........

".......I found myself working in the parcels office at East Croydon, but what a difference from small stations, where only parcels were dealt with, plus the occasional small animal. Here we charged up horses, all the

56 The Staff at Purley Oaks about 1906 (below)
Posed by the signal box, this group indicates how labour-intensive the railways once were. In the year 2001 no more than one person at a time works at Purley Oaks. In 1923 there were 38 signal boxes in the area now included in the borough of Croydon. None now remain, as signalling in the area is controlled from either Clapham Junction or Three Bridges.

animals of a circus, corpses, horses and sulkies going to trotting contests, theatrical scenery and mountains of P.L.A. (Passengers' Luggage in Advance). The day of the family car had not arrived, and motor coaches had solid tyres, so people travelled by train when on holiday. In 1919 there was still a restriction of one hundredweight on consignments by passenger train. This had been brought in because women porters had been employed during the war, in fact they were still there at that time. Many of the ticket collectors were women too......

".......the Chief Clerk of the station, Alfred Field was responsible for the booking office, parcels office and telegraph office. His pre-war salary was 47/6, while the senior booking clerk received 37/6.......Nearly all the old 'uns were heavy drinkers and wore heavy 'Old Bill' moustaches which were stained with tobacco and beer. Before the 1914 war they used to start their early duty with coffee laced with rum in the *Railway Arms*…..

".......One customer was the Rev. Wm. Wilks, Rector of Shirley, who was better known for raising the Shirley Poppy. That was our name for him, as he had some affliction which had caused his nose to spread and become purple. Another was Mr W.H. Still, J.P., who farmed a large part of Addington long before New Addington was thought of. Then there was Col. Daniels of Fairchildes, Lord of the Manor of Chelsham, who was decidedly peppery and living a couple of centuries too late. There were no buses to Shirley or Addington then and quite a number of people used to cycle in and deposit their machines in the left luggage office. We got to know many Shirley and Addington folk this way……..

"……..During my last years in the parcels office the claims clerk had long periods off sick, and I used to cover his duties. All claims for damage had to be investigated by inspection, and this duty took me into many interesting places. Apart from wholesale and retail premises, private houses had to be visited. These ranged from the pleasant villas of Addiscombe, and the larger houses of the well-to-do, to the slum quarters of Croydon. On one occasion I called at the home of Samuel Coleridge Taylor, where I met his son. After we had finished our business he showed me the scenes from *Hiawatha* which an artist had painted on the walls of the hall for his famous father, who died in 1909.

"I went to a house in an Old Town slum which has long since gone, and when I knocked a slatternly but friendly woman answered. I told her I had come to inspect a damaged tea service and she said 'Come in, mate. Don't take any notice of the place, I haven't had time to tidy up yet'. By the look of the house the last time it was tidy must have been during the Boer War. There were several small children and the sink was full of little potties. She asked me if I would like a cuppa, but I hastily said I had just had one. On another occasion I went to Wilford Road, where the costermongers used to live. At that time it was known as 'banghole'. At the house where I called a donkey looked out of the front room, while the open front door revealed the bannister rail and supports had long since been used as firewood......

".......In 1936 I transferred downstairs as stationmaster's clerk, where I had a whole lot of new duties to learn...... At first I felt lost, but gradually got used to it, and found it the most interesting job I ever had. At that time Fairfield Yard was still occupied by the Northern District Engineer's sidings and workshops, and the east side of the bridge which used to lead to Central Croydon station was easily identified where it had been bricked up. There were all sorts of trades being carried out in the various sheds and buildings, and a new station could be built from the resources gathered there………

"…..as soon as I had got to know every member of the staff and what duties they could cover, other than their own, it became easier for me to arrange alteration of duties when someone was absent sick or on leave. The station inspectors were a tower of strength in this respect. Preparation of paybills was a big job which kept me busy, and when P.A.Y.E. was

57 Thornton Heath Signal Box Interior - 1903
Most signal boxes would have looked similar from the early days of railways until modernisation with colour lights in the twentieth century. Even so, there are still many boxes like this in various parts of the country.

58 The Last of the Goods Horses - 1952
Horses were employed for shunting in goods yards and on local delivery work. Here Bert Andrews is with Tommy, his pal for 19 years, at East Croydon on the day the horses were replaced by motor vehicles in February 1952.

59 Taking Water - 1920
Most stations of any size had water columns to supply the needs of steam engines and scenes such as this at West Croydon were common. There was a locomotive shed on the left until 1935 when a new one was built at Norwood Junction to replace it. Note the overhead gantries for the original electrification. This is one of the late O.J. Morris's famous sepia prints. He was a resident of Beulah Hill and well-known for his excellent transport photography.

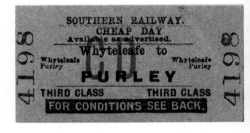

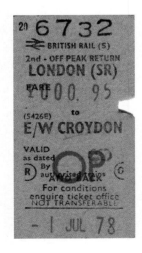

60 Steam Engine - 1939
This early colour photograph shows an 'N' class locomotive in Southern Railway green livery near Norwood Junction. It appears to have been taken from Tennison Road bridge, looking east.

introduced this made still more work. One thing which is forgotten now was the deduction of 2½% of everybody's pay in the late 1930s when the Southern Railway was having a lean time......

"......There were 58 sweetmeat machines on the station, some with eight columns. All were filled with penny items, except the two column Nestles machines, which sold penny milk chocolate bars and twopenny smokers chocolate, which was plain and slightly bitter. These machines were my responsibility, and I filled them during my lunch break. It was a very cold job in winter.

"In 1939, on the Sunday war with Germany was declared, I was on duty. When that siren went during the morning the Station Inspector was down the goods yard, so I instructed the train announcer to tell waiting passengers they could take shelter in the subway, if desired. There was a general movement there, and one old dear fainted. It turned out to be a false alarm, but afterwards, when such warnings were commonplace, everyone soon became used to them.

"An almost total blackout was imposed at first, only very faint blue lights being allowed in trains, which had to have all blinds down, and on station platforms. When the first Canadians arrived they proved to be a rough lot, and I soon had a thick file headed 'Damage by Canadian Soldiers'. One night a station foreman saw some Canadians loading something into a compartment of a Tattenham Corner train, and when he shone his hand-lamp he saw it was a two-column chocolate machine. Another night they dropped an eight-column machine on the down main track. The next train smashed it and the ballast was littered with packets of sweets and pennies".

Bill Tharby served in the Home Guard throughout the war and later worked at Redhill and then Waterloo before retiring after 50 years service on the railway.

61 Freight Train - 1938
An early colour photograph at Windmill Bridge junction, north of East Croydon. A freight train headed by a 'K' class locomotive is travelling south from Norwood Yard, at that time one of the most important marshalling yards on the Southern Railway.

62 Near Norwood Junction - May 1939
Looking north, one of three new English Electric diesel shunting engines built for the Southern Railway is in the foreground as a freight train heads north. On the far right is a suburban electric train on its way towards Croydon.

63 Near Waddon Marsh about 1929 (above)
The Wimbledon to West Croydon line retained much of the atmosphere of a country branch line until its closure in 1997 for incorporation in Tramlink. This photograph was taken from Purley Way bridge, looking north-west just before the line was electrified in 1930. Waddon Marsh New Siding, leading to Waddon Mill is on the left, protected by the gates.

64 Waddon Marsh - 29th August 1953 (below)
Looking south-east from Purley Way bridge, a two-car electric train leaves the passing loop at the halt. On the right are two of the gas works locomotives. An unusual feature between West Croydon and Beddington Lane was the single electrified track for passenger trains, and the adjacent single non-electrified track freight line, both used by trains in both directions.

65 Extract from Ordnance Survey Map (above right)
This is part of the 1933 with additions to 1938 edition of the 6 inches to the mile map, showing the gas and electricity works and sidings which even in the 1950s had some of the heaviest freight traffic on the Southern Region of British Railways. It is reproduced at a scale of approximately 9 inches to the mile.

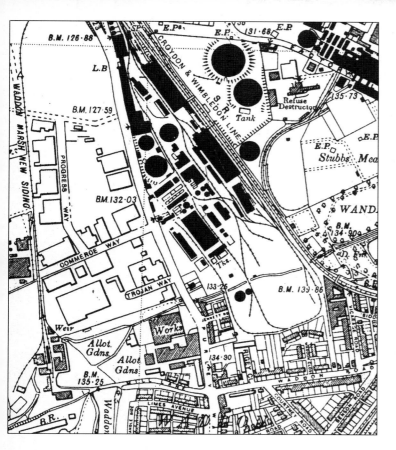

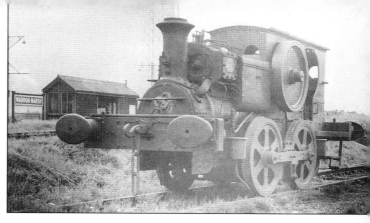

66 Gas Works Locomotive - 29th August 1953 (top right)

Allen Lambert, a rather quaint looking Aveling Porter industrial locomotive built in 1900, was a familiar feature of Croydon Gas Works from the days of the Croydon Gas Company.

67 Sentinel Locomotive - 29th August 1953 (above right)

Joyce, built in 1927, was another locomotive at the gas works.

68 Croydon 'B' Power Station - 27th August 1950 (below)

Croydon 'A' Power Station in Factory Lane had an electric locomotive worked from overhead wires. After the Second World War Croydon Corporation started construction of the 'B' power station to the west of Purley Way. With nationalisation of the electricity industry the power station was completed by the British Electricity Authority and two of its three new Peckett steam locomotives are seen here.

69 Norwood Locomotive Shed - 1953 (left)
A mixed selection of ex-London, Brighton and
South Coast, and Southern Railway
locomotives line up at the shed on a sunny day
a few years after nationalisation of the railways
in 1948. This locomotive shed was opened in
1935 to replace that at West Croydon, and
finally closed in 1964. Other sheds in the
borough were at Purley (South Eastern
Railway) opened in 1898 and closed in 1928,
and at Stoat's Nest (Coulsdon), opened in 1900
and also closed in 1928. There was also one at
Addiscombe in the nineteenth century.

70 Leaving Sanderstead - May 1962
(below left)
The Oxted line remained steam operated until
the 1960s. Here the 4.48pm Victoria to
Brighton via Uckfield train has just left
Sanderstead on a bright spring evening. Until
1955 the services on the line were irregular,
with trains to a variety of routes and
destinations. On Sundays the only down trains
left East Croydon at 8.58 am, 9.14 am, 10.53
am, 3.00 pm, 7.06 pm, 7.30 pm and 9.42 pm.
Of these only four called at Sanderstead and
five at Riddlesdown.

71 Electric Train - August 1967 (above right)
The Brighton main line was electrified in 1932
and most of the other lines in the area had
been electrified before the Second World War.
A train consisting of ex-Southern Railway
4-Lav sets is approaching South Croydon not
long before being replaced by new rolling
stock.

72 Crossing Riddlesdown Viaduct in 1959
(centre right)
After leaving South Croydon the Oxted line
climbs into the North Downs and on the way
to East Grinstead traverses three tunnels and
three lattice viaducts. In this photograph Battle
of Britain class locomotive, *Kenley* is crossing
Riddlesdown Viaduct with a Victoria to
Ardingly rambler's excursion in September
1959.

73 Diesel-Electric Train - August 1967 (right)
Diesel-electric multiple unit trains were
gradually introduced on the Oxted line from
June 1962. Here one in Southern Region green
livery approaches South Croydon. The line
between Sanderstead and East Grinstead was
electrified on 5th October 1987, but a few of
the diesel-electric multiple units remained in
use for the Oxted to Uckfield line services into
the twenty-first century.

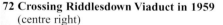

74 Purley Station - 1st January 1962 (left)
A Tattenham Corner to London Bridge train enters Purley on a bleak New Year's Day. The third-rail electrification system can suffer problems in severe winter weather as ice forms on the conductor rail. In very bad conditions it has been necessary for electric trains to be hauled by steam, and latterly diesel, locomotives. Heavy snowfalls in January 1987 left most of the railway lines in the district completely buried in snow and snow ploughs were in use locally for the first time in many years.

75 Electric Train - 13th August 1949
  (centre left)
A train of ex-London, Brighton and South Coast Railway coaches, as rebuilt by the Southern Railway, with a more modern trailer coach added, is approaching St. James's Junction on its way from West Croydon to Victoria via Crystal Palace. The tower of Gillett and Johnston's Bell Foundry is in the distance.

76 Freight Train - Early 1950s (below left)
A freight train headed by an ex-London, Brighton & South Coast Railway K class locomotive is about to pass under the splendid ex-Brighton signal gantry north of East Croydon. Steam engines tend to be remembered with affection and many are preserved in various parts of the country. They created a lot of smoke and dirt, however, as this photograph reminds us.

77 East Croydon - 6.26 pm on 23rd May
  1953 (above right)
East Croydon North signal box is to the right with Hall and Company's head offices beyond. The company had private sidings here worked by their own locomotive. The signal box and signals were replaced when new colour-light signals came into use in 1955.

Although electric trains were the norm at this time, two steam-hauled passenger trains and a light engine are in this photograph taken by the late John Price, a well-known transport historian who lived locally for many years. Leaving the station northbound and hauled by a Schools class locomotive, is the 2.42 pm Margate to Cannon Street train. This set off in an easterly direction along the coast and pursued a circuitous and leisurely course via Dover, Folkestone, Tonbridge, Redhill and Croydon to arrive in Cannon Street about four hours later! It even stopped at such unlikely places as Purley, Norwood Junction and Forest Hill.

The southbound train is the 6.10 pm Victoria to Brighton. This split at East Croydon, the front part running fast to Oxted and then on to Brighton. The rear four coaches had a different engine attached and ran slow to Oxted and Tunbridge Wells West.

78 West Croydon - 15th March 1967
  (below right)
Looking towards London at 12.30 pm, a 2-EPB unit Wimbledon branch train is standing in the bay platform on the left. The signal is clear for the 4-EPB unit train on the right to leave for Sutton and Wimbledon via St Helier.

79 Coulsdon North - 24th October 1980
At the end of the nineteenth century the Brighton company built a new line avoiding Redhill, which for many years had been a source of delays on the main line. Known as the Quarry Line it included widening to four tracks south of South Croydon to a terminus for local trains at Coulsdon, initially taking the name Stoat's Nest and opening on 5th November 1899. The station was renamed Coulsdon and Smitham Downs after a serious accident in 1909. It became Coulsdon West for a few weeks in 1923, then Coulsdon North. The station was closed in 1983.

80 Addiscombe - 10th March 1995
Electric services began on the Addiscombe branch on 28th February 1926. During later years through services to London generally ceased, a shuttle service running from Elmers End. In 1993, the depot, seen on the right, closed and new 'Networker' trains such as this provided the service. The signal box was the last manual one in the area and was destroyed by fire in 1996, over a year before the line and station closed on 31st May 1997. The line has been incorporated into Tramlink between its former junction at Blackhorse Lane and Elmers End.

81 Connex Train at South Croydon - July 1998
From 1989 railway services in the area were part of Network South East. Following privatisation, a French Company, Connex South Central took over responsibility for many local services. Their bright, (though difficult to keep clean), livery is well shown in this picture of a class 319 unit speeding southwards near South Croydon.

82 Bingham Road - 28th July 1980

Passenger traffic and services on the Woodside and South Croydon line gradually declined until only a few trains remained, running a shuttle service during peak hours only between Sanderstead or Selsdon and Elmers End. Eventually the line was closed on 13th May 1983. Bingham Road Station had first opened on 1st September 1906, closing with the line on 15th March 1915. It was rebuilt and reopened when the line was electrified on 30th September 1935. Usually known in the locality as Bingham Halt it retained a 'Southern Electric' sign until the day after this photograph was taken.

83 Bingham Road - 10th May 2001

When Tramlink was planned it was decided to remove the embankments (the bridges here had already been demolished) so that a tram stop could be provided at street level for easy access. The stop, now called Addiscombe, is a little north of the previous station, between Lower Addiscombe and Bingham Roads. A tram is seen here crossing Bingham Road at the same place as the train above.

84 Selhurst Train Care Depot from the Air - 26th May 1999 (below)

This view illustrates the large area of land occupied by the railway depot and tracks in this area. Tennison Road Bridge is in the left foreground. The next road crossing of the tracks is at Windmill Bridge, just right of top centre on the main line, or Gloucester and Sydenham Road bridges on the West Croydon line (right).

85 Workmen - Croydon about 1900 (above)
Until the late nineteenth/early twentieth century manual work was one of the main forms of employment. Labour was plentiful and cheap, and hours long. Here a gang of workmen, apparently engaged on road works, pose for the photographer. The location is not recorded.

86 Steam-Roller - Late 1880s (centre left)
Croydon Corporation bought this Aveling Porter steam roller in 1886. As roads were improved equipment such as this became essential.

87 Steam-Roller - 22nd September 1951
(below left)
The same steam-roller was photographed by John Meredith at the Corporation's Gillett Road Depot in Thornton Heath over 60 years later. Apart from minor alterations it was still recognisably the same vehicle. It remained in service into the 1960s as the oldest working steam-roller in the country and is now in the collection of the Science Museum. This is an excellent example of well-constructed equipment having a very long and useful life - something that rarely happens in modern times.

88 Cartoon - 1897 (opposite right)
This cartoon was published in the *Croydon Society Gossip* of the 8th September 1897. At that time there was some local agitation for the widening of North End and George Street to ease traffic congestion, by demolishing the Whitgift Hospital, which has been drawn here without its pitched roof. There was equally a large body of opinion wanting the historic building preserved, which fortunately prevailed.

The Roads

In Croydon the general pattern of roads was well established by the time of the Croydon Inclosure Act of 1797. This provided for the enclosure of the common lands in the parish and appointed Commissioners who awarded the land and defined the highways as this extract illustrates.

"And we have appointed and staked out One Public Carriage Road of the width of Forty feet, called the Whitehorse Road, beginning at the north east end of a certain ancient lane called Newgate Lane, and leading north-eastward in a straight line over Croydon Common to an ancient gate called Whitehorse Gate.

"Also one other Public Carriage Road of the same width called Windmill Road, and Lane's Road, beginning at the east end of another lane near Broad Green and leading on the south-east side of Croydon Windmill along the present gravel road, across the Whitehorse Road to Dragnell's Wood, then turning northward towards Selhurst Lane, to an ancient gate called Selhurst Gate".

Newgate Lane is now called Wellesley Road, and Lane's Road is now Northcote Road. The width of the roads (which would include the present pavements) as laid out in the commissioners' award is in many cases unchanged over the last two hundred years, although one or two seem to be slightly narrower in places than laid down in the award!

When the railways were built they generally provided bridges to carry existing roads under or over the tracks and with few exceptions all the present railway/road bridges date back to the building of the railway, although most have now been reconstructed, and in some cases widened.

There were a few level crossings, such as at Stoats Nest, and Waddon Marsh Lane but most railway crossings were by means of bridges. The only completely new road crossing places provided since the railways were first built are thought to be Tennison Road, South Norwood (around 1880) and Fairfield Bridge (Barclay Road) which replaced a footbridge carrying the ancient Fairfield Footpath in 1956. The pattern of roads laid down long before the railways came has thus influenced later building development and the lack of new roads across the railways continues to have a considerable impact on the traffic flows of today.

The Turnpikes were, as mentioned elsewhere, abolished by 1872 and road conditions were generally poor during the latter part of the nineteenth century, even in towns as can be seen in illustration number 99 on page 46. *Croydon Society Gossip* included the following comment in its issue of 29th September 1897.

"That the roads of Croydon are in a very bad state from one end of the borough to the other, no one who has either lived in the town, or merely passed through it will be slow to assert. But some roads are in a very much worse state than others, and the aggravating part of it is that it is those very roads which are of the most importance, both from the residential and the business point of view, that are in the worse state. It would be impossible - in the vicinity of London, at any rate - to find a more disgracefully maintained thoroughfare than North End or George Street, and the main streets of South Norwood and Thornton Heath are practically as bad. The name of Croydon has become a by-word because of its filthy, founderous, dangerous streets".

The horse was still supreme on the roads throughout the nineteen century, although there were early attempts to use steam traction for road vehicles. Walter Hancock, amongst others, had some success with his steam carriages, and used them between Bank and Paddington in London as well as on excursions to Brighton, so they were probably seen passing through Croydon occasionally. But for the most part it was a world of horses. Croydon was reasonably well served by stage-coaches and horse buses (see page 55), but most people had to walk unless they had their own horse or carriage or could afford train fares.

Cycling developed after the 1860s. In 1869 John Mayall made the first attempt to ride to Brighton on a 'boneshaker' but only managed to reach Redhill. By the 1880s the 'ordinary' or 'penny-farthing' bicycle had become popular, with the 'safety' cycle emerging into very much its present form by the 1890s when there was a boom in cycling for pleasure and work purposes.

Traction engines and steam-rollers were allowed to use the highway under legislation from 1860 and 1880. Motor cars had been appearing on the roads in small numbers for a few years but could only be used under the same laws and all had to be preceded by a man walking with a red flag, and travel at no more than 4mph. In 1896 a new act enabled them to travel at speeds up to 12 mph and without a man walking in front. Speed limits were rigidly enforced but as motor vehicles improved and became more reliable the restrictions were relaxed.

Traffic and congestion grew inexorably throughout the twentieth century. Road accidents were at a very high level by the 1920s and much needed traffic regulations and road improvements were gradually introduced after this. White lines were painted on roads from 1925 onwards, but in 1927 national road accidents totalled more than 130,000, with over 5,000 people killed, many more than today. From 1931 traffic lights were introduced following successful trials in London, but it was not until 1934 that driving tests were introduced.

A by-pass for Croydon was discussed as early as 1908 and eventually Purley Way was constructed, opening in 1924. It was one of the first by-pass roads and now needs its own by-pass! At the beginning of the twenty-first century traffic congestion and environmental pollution caused by the ever increasing number of road vehicles is a major problem with no easy solutions.

THE CROWN HILL DEATH TRAP.

89 A Heavy Load in the 1890s (above)
A large block of stone such as this needed three horses to move it. F. Stephens' East Surrey Monumental & Steam Masonry Works was in Brighton Road between Bartlett Street and Drover's Road. Most of the staff appear to have turned out for the photographer.

90 Horses in Lodge Road about 1900
(centre left)
Scenes such as this would have been very common before the First World War when the horse was the prime means of transport in towns.

91 A Pony and Trap - 8th July 1896
(left)
W.E. Wilson had several shops and cafes in and around Croydon from the 1890s until the 1970s and the name is still remembered with affection by older Croydonians. Horse and trade shows were once common and many businesses took a real pride in the appearance of their animals and vehicles. This turnout won First Prize and Champion Tradesmen's Lass in 108 entries at the Third Horse, Pony and Donkey Parade in 1896. It also won First Prize in the Tradesmen's Turnouts at the Croydon show on 17th June of the same year.

92 Smithy at Woodside - 1894 (above)
William Bell's smithy was the last building in Woodside village on the north side of the street just before the green and near the site later occupied by the war memorial. William Bell was the farrier from about 1880 until 1937. Such smithies were a very common and necessary part of life when horses were the main means of transport.

93 William Waters Advertisement - 1876
  (right)
Carriage building was at one time a major industry in the town. As this advert suggests, Croydon Basket Carriages were once famous. As time went on many carriage builders turned to building bodies for motor vehicles as well, eventually concentrating on the new form of transport.

WILLIAM WATERS,

(Late WATERS & SON),

Carriage Builder and Harness Maker,

5, GEORGE STREET,

CROYDON,

Having succeeded to the above business, respectfully thanks his numerous Customers and the Public generally, for the liberal support so many years extended to the late Firm, and hopes, by strict attention to all orders entrusted to his care, to merit a continuance of their favours.

EVERY DESCRIPTION OF

LIGHT MODERN CARRIAGES, CARTS,

&c., &c.,

ON SALE OR BUILT TO ORDER.

ESTIMATES GIVEN FOR REPAIRS.

CARRIAGES LENT ON HIRE WITH OPTION OF PURCHASE.

THE
ORIGINAL CROYDON BASKET CARRIAGE MANUFACTORY.

94 Penny-Farthing Bicycle about 1887
Photographed in the garden of number 3, High Street, South Norwood this splendid view illustrates both the size of the large wheel and the costume which cyclists adopted in the late Victorian period. Cycling soon became very popular with both sexes and numerous cycling clubs were formed.

95 Tradesmen's Tricycle about 1896
W.E. Wilson not only used horse power for his deliveries but human power as well. The lad is very smart but his riding position looks to be somewhat precarious and the steering mechanism not too responsive!

96 Onward Steam Cycle Works (right) **and
97 Onward Motor & Cycle Works**
     (centre right)
These two views illustrate the way in which a
small company could adapt to the development
of new inventions. First recorded in the local
directory for 1891, the cycle works of C.F.
Miles had within a few years become a motor
and cycle works to deal with the increasing
number of motor vehicles appearing on the
roads. This building was adjacent to the
Windsor Castle public house in the Brighton
Road but by 1907 the firm had moved to the
other corner of Brantwood Road where it
remained in family ownership until the 1980s.

98 An Early *Chenard et Walcker* **Motor Car
     about 1904**
This postcard view is thought to show Bremner
Frith and family, who lived in St James's Road.
Registration numbers for motor vehicles were
introduced in 1904 and were issued by county
and county borough authorities. As a county
borough, Croydon was initially allocated the
letters BY, and later OY, RK and VB, which it
retained until ceasing to be a vehicle licensing
authority on becoming a London borough in
1965.

99 North End in 1896 (above)
Looking south from the corner of Poplar Walk this view demonstrates the appalling state of the roads even at the end of the Victorian era. The tram track area is paved with setts or cobbles, and there is a cobbled street crossing in the foreground. This would normally have been kept reasonably clean by a crossing-sweeper. Otherwise the road surface has many potholes and looks to be very dirty and dusty. See comment on page 41.

100 Emancipation Day - 1896 (centre left)
On Saturday 14th November 1896, the Locomotives on Highways Act came into force. It removed the requirement for a man to walk in front of a mechanically propelled vehicle, and raised the maximum speed limit from four to 12 miles per hour. *Croydon Society Gossip* for 18th November included the following report. "The initial procession of motor cars to Brighton on Saturday drew a record crowd into the main streets of Croydon. The procession, which on starting from the Hotel Metropole included close upon 100 vehicles, numbered less than 50 on reaching Croydon, and passed through the town by the main London road from Norbury to Purley. London Road, North End, High Street, and South End were packed with excited crowds, whose numbers were far in excess of those which turned out on the occasion of the recent Royal visit....... The smell was disagreeable in the extreme; so much so to induce an evening contemporary to break forth into song with the words 'Stinkle, stinkle, little car'..........It is difficult to realise the enormous changes in our system of living that will shortly be brought about by the introduction of motor cars. To begin with it is extremely probable that the

railway companies will suffer. People to whom time is no object will travel about in their own motor carriages and a journey of a hundred miles in a day will be accomplished quite easily. It follows too, as a matter of course, that as soon as the high roads are used once more by travellers, the wayside inns will come in for a spell of prosperity. In course of time railway refreshment rooms will become scarce, and the railway ham sandwich quite extinct. The old-fashioned coaching-houses will be freshly painted, and the long low-ceiled room will be haunted once more by the smell of many luncheons".

In this photograph one of the cars in the procession has just passed West Croydon station and is being driven along North End.

101 Hansom Cab in the early 1900s
(below left)
A hansom cab stands in the forecourt of Purley station.

102 A Breakdown at South Croydon around 1908 (above)
Early motor vehicles were extremely unreliable and breakdowns were common. Here a postcard published by a local photographer shows a Royal Mail motor van which has broken down near the *Red Deer* in the Brighton Road. Real horse power has been summoned to assist, and a small crowd of interested onlookers is enjoying the spectacle.

103 The Half Moon Garage around 1910
(centre right)
This garage was alongside the *Half Moon* public house in London Road at Broad Green. It seems to have been established in stables formerly belonging to the public house. The old hay loft is in the centre.

104 Tradesman's Hand-Cart about 1910
(right)
This baker's hand-cart is typical of many in use in the days when nearly all tradesmen offered home deliveries.

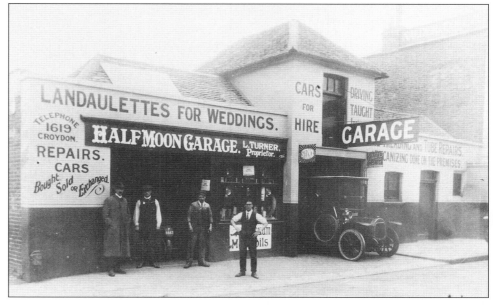

105 Chapman's Advertisement about 1920
(left)
The charges shown here seem to be rather
expensive considering general costs and wage
levels at the time.

**106 Motor Cycle Rally - Sunday 9th March
1912** (above)
Motor cycles were becoming popular during the
Edwardian period. Club rallies often assembled
on the forecourt of the *Swan and Sugar Loaf* as
here when the Motor Cycle Union Spring Rally
from Croydon to Tunbridge Wells and back was
creating a lot of interest. The vehicle on the left
with the wickerwork body appears to be a
Chater-Lea cycle car.

108 Waterman's Works - late 1920s (above)
Waterman's Dyeing and Cleaning Works were in Purley Way from the mid-1920s. This fleet of locally built Trojan vans was used for their collection and delivery service. Note the splendid uniforms worn by the drivers and the immaculate condition of the vehicles.

107 Garage - Tamworth Road about 1925
(left)
Moore's Presto garage and workshop was in Tamworth Road backing on to their office in North End. The car on the left is a Napier and on the right is a Sunbeam. The chauffeurs look very smart.

109 Pedestrian Signals at Norbury - 1932
(right)
The inauguration of the first traffic signals operated by pedestrians in this country obviously was a matter of great interest. The *Croydon Advertiser* reported that "the Mayor, Alderman William Peet, pressed the button to stop traffic amid cheers and excited cries."

Traffic signals were first introduced in the United Kingdom in the 1930s. Pedestrian crossings with Belisha Beacons (named after Mr Hore-Belisha) first appeared around 1934.

110 Brighton Road, Purley about 1930
(above)
Looking south from the tram terminus, Godstone Road is on the left and Banstead Road on the right. Telegraph poles still lined the road and gas lighting remained. A policeman controlled the relatively light traffic at this busy junction, now known as Purley Cross. The van is a Saurer.

111 Steam wagon about 1937 (left)
In common with many local authorities Croydon Corporation owned a number of steam wagons for heavy work. One of them was being used here on tree-felling operations in Addiscombe Road.

112 Gravel Hill - 8th September 1934
(below left)
Looking south, the narrow lane would within a few years lose its rural appearance and be transformed into a dual carriageway. Road widening schemes totally changed many of the country lanes around the town as housing development spread, and road traffic increased. Gravel Hill tram stop is now on the right and many of the fields in the distance have been built on.

113 Marlpit Lane - 14th June 1937

Marlpit Lane was another road to be widened in the 1930s to take increasing traffic. The old brick-arch railway bridge was being removed and a new steel bridge was ready to be rolled into position a couple of weeks later.

114 Hartley Hill, Purley - 27th March 1956
(centre right)

Many suburban roads remained unadopted by the local authority until some time after the houses were completed. This is an example demonstrating that some road surfaces were very poor even in the 1950s. A few unmade and unadopted roads still remain in Croydon.

115 Wellesley Road - 28th February 1969
(below)

Photographed looking north from the then new Whitgift Centre multi-storey car park, the alignment and width of the old road was virtually unchanged from the days of the Enclosure Award at the end of the eighteenth century. This was soon to be altered as the new dual carriageway works were by this time well under way. It was at the time intended to continue the dual carriageway up to Spurgeon's Bridge, and to widen St James's Road to Broad Green, and Sumner Road from there to Mitcham Road, completing the proposed inner-ring road. Changed attitudes to road schemes resulted in this northern section being abandoned.

116 North End in the mid 1960s (above)
Parking meters were introduced in Croydon on
2nd October 1961. Traffic congestion had
increased as car ownership and use went up.
The bad conditions in North End, especially on
a Saturday afternoon are well-illustrated by
this photograph. A general desire to reduce
congestion, pollution and fumes led Croydon
Council to first introduce a partial
pedestrianisation scheme, then a complete ban
on traffic in North End. It is now a much more
attractive place in which to stroll and shop.

117 Roads Protest 1990 (left)
Proposals for most new road schemes
generally lost public support by the 1990s as
the environmental impact became
unacceptable. This public rally against a
widening scheme in the Norbury area was
firmly in favour of public transport
improvements.

118 Macclesfield Road, South Norwood about 1910 (above)
and 119 - on 11th May 2001 (below)

These two photographs highlight the great changes that have taken place in many suburban streets since the Second World War. Photographed from Estcourt Road, the grocery shop of W. Skinner on the corner of Albert Road (left) eventually closed, presumably because so many local residents were getting cars and using supermarkets for their shopping.

The shop part of the premises has been converted into living accommodation. The road is now lined with parked cars because the terraced houses have no space for garages. The attractive iron railings on the low walls in front of the houses were removed in aid of the war effort around 1940. However the houses have not changed greatly and over ninety years later the street is still recognisable.

120 Wagonette about 1890 (above)
Wagonettes were used extensively for party outings. The interesting point about this photograph is that the vehicle has destination boards on the side, suggesting that it may have been used on some sort of regular service. However on this particular occasion it seems to be a party trip which has stopped at, or is starting from, the *Purley Arms* in the Brighton Road. Note the cornet player, which suggests a fairly noisy time was in prospect.

121 Motor Bus - 1903 (centre left)
Reports of Croydon's first motor bus service appeared in local papers early in 1903. One report dated 21st February said "A motor car service has been established between the corner of Carshalton Road and East Croydon, and is evidently doing very well. Another car, it is reported, is being constructed for the service". But the *Croydon Times* of the same date reported "It is as noisy as a waggon loosely filled with biscuit boxes. It is unsightly and combines nearly every feature that a public vehicle should not possess".

The vehicle was a Milnes-Daimler registered in the name of William Warsany, of 38 Tamworth Road, Croydon. A second vehicle had been delivered by March. There were several Police Court cases involving the buses and on 3rd May the owner and driver were charged with furious driving at Carshalton Hill - at 13 miles per hour!

This photograph shows one of the vehicles turning into Tamworth Road from North End. The buses ran between Croydon and Sutton for about a year, after which they were sold to the London and South Western Railway Company to run between Exeter and Chagford, and later went to work in Newport Docks for some years.

Buses

Croydon's position on the Brighton Road about 10 miles from London meant that it was ideally placed as a posting station for stage coaches which generally needed to change horses about every ten miles. It was therefore linked with the metropolis by public transport at quite an early date. A War Office survey of 1756 records that the town could provide 781 guest beds and stabling for 1,220 horses, by far the largest number in the County of Surrey. The principal inns were the *Crown, George, Greyhound,* and *Green Dragon.*

A short stage-coach service appears to have been operated by John Windham around 1681, with one journey each way daily between Croydon and Southwark via Brixton. A stage-coach service through Croydon was recorded as early as 1760 and by 1825 five coaches were providing short stage services between the *Crown* Inn and the City. The longer distance coaches had by then become more frequent but records are sparse. However by the 1830s there seem to have been about 25 coaches each way through the town. An 1839 Directory shows coaches and omnibuses between Croydon and London 'continually throughout the day', and longer distance coaches to and from Brighton, Eastbourne, East Grinstead, Lewes and Reigate. The longer distance coaches were eventually withdrawn because of competition from the railways. The last regular stage-coaches on the Brighton Road ceased in October 1887.

The short distance coaches became omnibuses over time. With the opening of the London and Croydon Railway in 1839, an omnibus service, probably the town's first local route, started running between West Croydon station and Mitcham, connecting with the trains. Local omnibus services developed slowly and references to them are few. The London General Omnibus Company was formed in 1856 and it took over one bus service between Croydon and

Oxford Street in that year.

There is a record in 1866 of the South Eastern Railway or a contractor on its behalf, operating a service between Addiscombe Road Station and Croydon High Street, worked by a 'well appointed omnibus, which meets nearly all the trains. Single fare, inside or outside - 3d! In real terms this was probably equivalent to £3 or £4 today. The level of fare for a relatively short distance suggests that passengers would in general have been from the better-off classes!

The first motor bus service in the town was introduced in 1903, to run between East Croydon station and Sutton. It lasted only a year. In February 1905 Thomas Tilling Ltd demonstrated one of their Milnes-Daimler double deck buses locally, and in March 1906 invited guests, including representatives of the local press to a demonstration trip from the Crystal Palace to Streatham, Norbury, Thornton Heath and back up the hills to the Crystal Palace.

The second regular motor bus service in the town was run by the London Motor Omnibus Company trading as Vanguard (see illustration below). This company was amalgamated with the London General Omnibus Company in July 1908. Early motor buses were notoriously unreliable and between August 1908 and March 1909 there were reports of 277 instances of derelict omnibuses blocking tramlines in the town.

As motor buses became more reliable so the services expanded. The introduction of the famous 'B' type by the General company saw their services expanding in the area and from 1916 Thomas Tilling Ltd., by agreement with the General company also became a major local operator.

In 1921 the General company reached an agreement with the East Surrey Traction Company of Reigate over bus operation in the North Downs area. A temporary wartime Act had

given highway authorities some control over bus services in their area and Croydon Corporation used this means to prevent the entry of new bus routes. The Act lapsed on 15th August 1921 and the East Surrey company introduced routes from Croydon to Sevenoaks, Edenbridge and Redhill the very next day. Other routes were soon started to Guildford, Dorking, Uckfield and Hartfield.

As the network of bus routes grew, so areas away from the railway stations became more accessible and saw increased house building. This applied particularly on the higher ground around Croydon in places such as Sanderstead, Selsdon, Old Coulsdon and Shirley.

The East Surrey Traction Company assumed control of many bus routes north of London in 1932 and was as a result renamed London General Country Services Ltd. All bus services in Croydon, together with the local tramways, came under the control of the newly formed London Passenger Transport Board from 1st July 1933.

Meanwhile in 1930 Green Line Coaches had been set up as a wholly owned subsidiary of the London General Omnibus Company. Several of its long-distance services ran through Croydon, and with a temporary break due to the war, continued to serve the town into the 1980s. The 726 service between Bromley and Heathrow is the only local surviving relic of the once flourishing routes. Some Southdown, and later, National Express coach services have for many years run between London and the south coast along Purley Way, picking up passengers locally only at Thornton Heath Pond, Waddon, Purley and Coulsdon.

Until the 1980s London Transport was virtually the only bus operator in the district but privatisation has led to more operators appearing on the scene, albeit under the overall planning control of London Transport, or as recently set up, a new organisation known as Transport for London (T/L).

22 Horse Bus - 1905 (below left)
The Sutton motor bus service was soon replaced by a regular horse bus route from Woodside, and later West Croydon, operated by the Star Omnibus Company Limited. This was quite a large company based in London, which in 1904 owned 263 buses and 2,185 horses. The Sutton service seems to have ceased in 1906 when the electric trams started running between Croydon and Sutton.

123 Vanguard Motor Bus - 1908 (right)
A regular motor bus service between Croydon and Oxford Street started in 1908. It was run by the Vanguard Company which introduced route numbers to London and in July 1908 had been absorbed by the London General Omnibus Company. This photograph shows one of their buses in South End, probably waiting to get on to its stand in the forecourt of the *Swan and Sugar Loaf* Hotel. Route 3 ran to Croydon only until September 1909.

Bourne and Balmer's Coaches
124 About 1925 (above) **125 About 1936**
(centre) **and 126 Summer 1955** (below)
These three photographs illustrate the way in which vehicle design changed over a period of around thirty years. Bourne and Balmer ran regular coach services between Croydon and destinations on the coast, as well as providing a private hire service for parties. This carried on the tradition started by the jobmasters with their wagonettes, and possibly even the stage-coach proprietors.

The company was first recorded as Removal Contractors in the local directory for 1924. From about 1933 their coach station in Dingwall Road was used as a garage and provided the departure point for their tours etc. After the Second World War the company was acquired by Timpson's of Catford, and that company in turn became part of National Travel. The coach station was rebuilt in the 1960s, but is no longer in use. Other companies in the area providing regular coach services and private hire coaches at various times included Bennett's of Shirley, John Bennett's of London Road, Taylors, Woodside coaches and Homeland Tours.

**127 Bus Garage Under Construction -
11th October 1915** (above)
Croydon bus garage in the Brighton Road was
nearing completion when this photograph was
taken. The garage was built by the London
General Omnibus Company who had an
agreement with Thomas Tilling Limited in
respect of certain operating arrangements. This
included providing garages for Tilling's use
and Croydon Garage was used by that
company from its opening in January 1916
until taken over by the newly formed London
Passenger Transport Board in 1933. In 1941
two bombs fell on the garage and almost
completely destroyed it with 65 buses. It was
rebuilt in the 1950s and is now owned by
Arriva London South which still uses the
garage code TC on its vehicles - standing for
Tilling's Croydon.

128 Tree Pruning - 1920 (centre right)
This photograph was taken at 2.0 pm on 4th
May 1920 and shows one of the General
company's famous 'B' type buses on tree
pruning duties in Crown Lane, Upper
Norwood, almost opposite the British Home
for Incurables. As can be seen, at that time
parts of the area were still rural and the road
was extremely narrow. Overhanging branches
were a danger to passengers on open-top
buses. Tree pruning still has to be carried out
to avoid damage to double deck vehicles and
their passengers.

129 Tilling Bus about 1920 (below right)
Looking south in Godstone Road on a sunny
day, the Kenley Hotel is on the right and
Riddlesdown on the left. One of Thomas
Tilling's TTA 1 Petrol Electric buses is on
route 59[A] from Caterham to Camden Town.
Note the lack of other traffic.

   Some 25 years later during the Second
World War, route 197 which then ran along
this stretch of road, was operated for some
months by ST type buses with gas trailers, as a
petrol saving measure.

130 At the Swan & Sugar Loaf - 31st March 1927 (above)
Here two General 'K' type open-top buses on route 54A and two Tilling TS3A Petrol Electric buses on route 34 were standing on the forecourt of the *Swan and Sugar Loaf* Hotel. The Inspector on the left was checking his time sheet while one of the drivers was examining his engine and another crew was enjoying a well-earned rest before starting the next journey.

131 The Red Deer about 1922 (below)
A southbound tram had just passed as a new Tilling Petrol Electric TS3A on route 12A departed for Oxford Circus. On the public house forecourt were two buses on route 75; on the left is a TTA1 which were all withdrawn by October 1922, and on the right what looks like a TTA2. Note the smart white summer coat of the driver filling his radiator, and the horse trough to supply necessary refreshment for the many horses still working hard.

132 George Street about 1930 (above)
Passengers board a 'K' type bus on route 12A as an 'NS' type bus on the short route 178 passes. This route replaced the Addiscombe trams from 1927 and by this time the 'NS' buses had been fitted with covered tops. However glass windscreens were not permitted in the London area because of objections from the Metropolitan Police. It was not until 1931 that they were allowed, and pneumatic tyres had only been fitted to buses and lorries from the late 1920s. A fixed stop is on the right. Most bus stop positions in suburban areas were not fixed or marked by posts and flags until the late 1930s/early 1940s.

133 East Croydon Station about 1931 (below)
The station building seen here was familiar to passengers for over ninety years from the mid 1890s until about 1990. One of Thomas Tilling's new ST type buses on route 12A was on its way to Oxford Circus in this view.

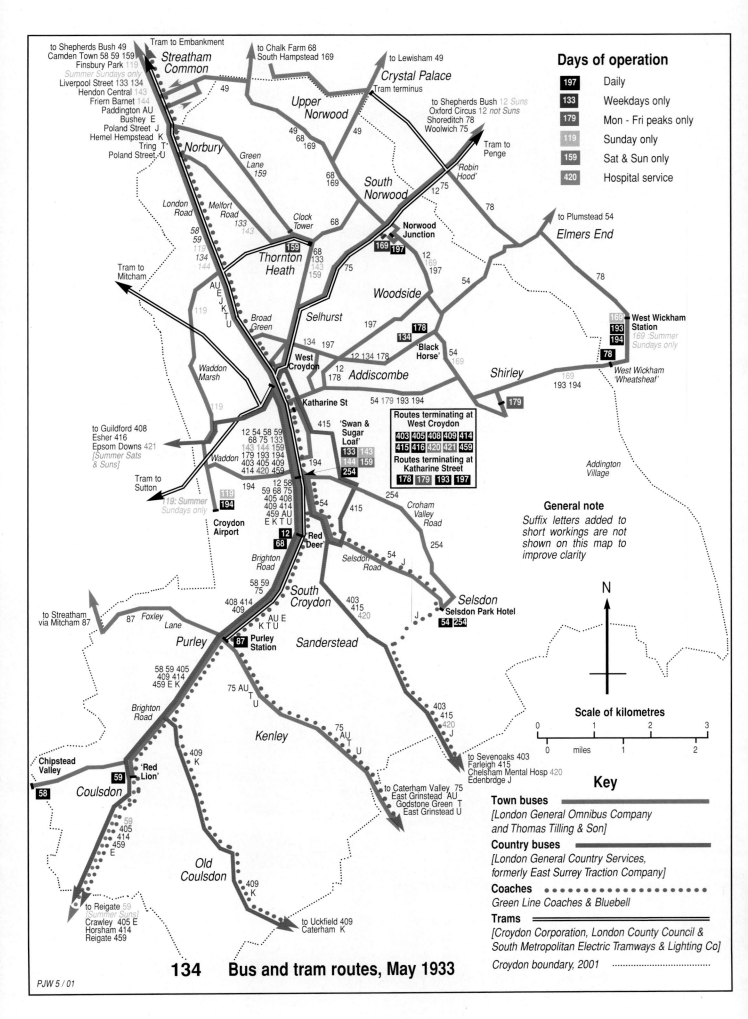

Days of operation

197	Daily
133	Weekdays only
179	Mon - Fri peaks only
119	Sunday only
159	Sat & Sun only
420	Hospital service

to Shepherds Bush 49
Camden Town 58 59 159
Finsbury Park 119
Summer Sundays only
Liverpool Street 133 134
Hendon Central 143
Friern Barnet 144
Paddington AU
Bushey E
Poland Street J
Hemel Hempstead K
Tring T
Poland Street U

Tram to Embankment

Streatham Common

to Chalk Farm 68
South Hampstead 169

to Lewisham 49

Crystal Palace
Tram terminus

to Shepherds Bush 12 *Suns*
Oxford Circus 12 *not Suns*
Shoreditch 78
Woolwich 75

Upper Norwood

Tram to Penge

49

Norbury

Green Lane 159

49 68 169

49

'Robin Hood'

Tram to Mitcham

London Road

Melfort Road 133 *143*

58 59 *119* 134 *144*

Clock Tower

68 169

South Norwood

12 75

78

to Plumstead 54

Elmers End

159

Thornton Heath

68 133 *143* 159

Norwood Junction

169 **197**

75

12 *169* 197

54

Broad Green

68

Selhurst

197

Woodside

119

AU E J K T U

134 197

West Croydon

12 134 178

178 **134**

'Black Horse'

54 *169*

169

West Wickham Station

169 **193** **194**

169 :Summer Sundays only

78

Waddon Marsh

119

197

12 178

Addiscombe

54

Shirley

193 194

West Wickham 'Wheatsheaf'

Katharine St

54 179 193 194

179

to Guildford 408
Esher 416
Epsom Downs 421
[Summer Sats & Suns]

415

'Swan & Sugar Loaf'

133 **143** **144** **159**

Addington Village

Waddon

12 54 58 59
68 75 133
143 144 159
179 193 194
403 405 409
414 420 459

194

Routes terminating at West Croydon
403 **405** **408** **409** **414**
415 **416** **420** **421** **459**

Routes terminating at Katharine Street
178 **179** **193** **197**

Tram to Sutton

119

119: Summer Sundays only

119 **194**

Croydon Airport

12 58
59 68 75
405 408
409 414
459 AU
E K T U

194

54

415

254

Croham Valley Road

254

General note
Suffix letters added to short workings are not shown on this map to improve clarity

12 **68**

'Red Deer'

Brighton Road

Selsdon Road

54 J

254

403 415 *420*

Selsdon

Selsdon Park Hotel

54 **254**

J

58 59 75

South Croydon

N

408 414 409

AU E K T U

to Streatham via Mitcham 87

87

Foxley Lane

87

Sanderstead

Scale of kilometres

0   1   2   3

0   miles   1   2

Purley

87 Purley Station

58 59 405
409 414
459 E K

75 AU T U

Kenley

75 AU T U

75 AU T U

403 415 *420* J

to Sevenoaks 403
Farleigh 415
Chelsham Mental Hosp 420
Edenbrdge J

Brighton Road

Chipstead Valley

59 'Red Lion'

58

Coulsdon

409 K

59 405 414 459 E

to Caterham Valley 75
East Grinstead AU
Godstone Green T
East Grinstead U

Old Coulsdon

409 K

59 to Reigate *[Summer Suns]*

Crawley 405 E
Horsham 414
Reigate 459

409 K

to Uckfield 409
Caterham K

Key

Town buses
[London General Omnibus Company and Thomas Tilling & Son]

Country buses
[London General Country Services, formerly East Surrey Traction Company]

Coaches ∙∙∙∙∙∙∙∙∙∙∙∙∙∙∙∙
Green Line Coaches & Bluebell

Trams
[Croydon Corporation, London County Council & South Metropolitan Electric Tramways & Lighting Co]

Croydon boundary, 2001 ∙∙∙∙∙∙∙∙∙∙∙

134   **Bus and tram routes, May 1933**

PJW 5 / 01

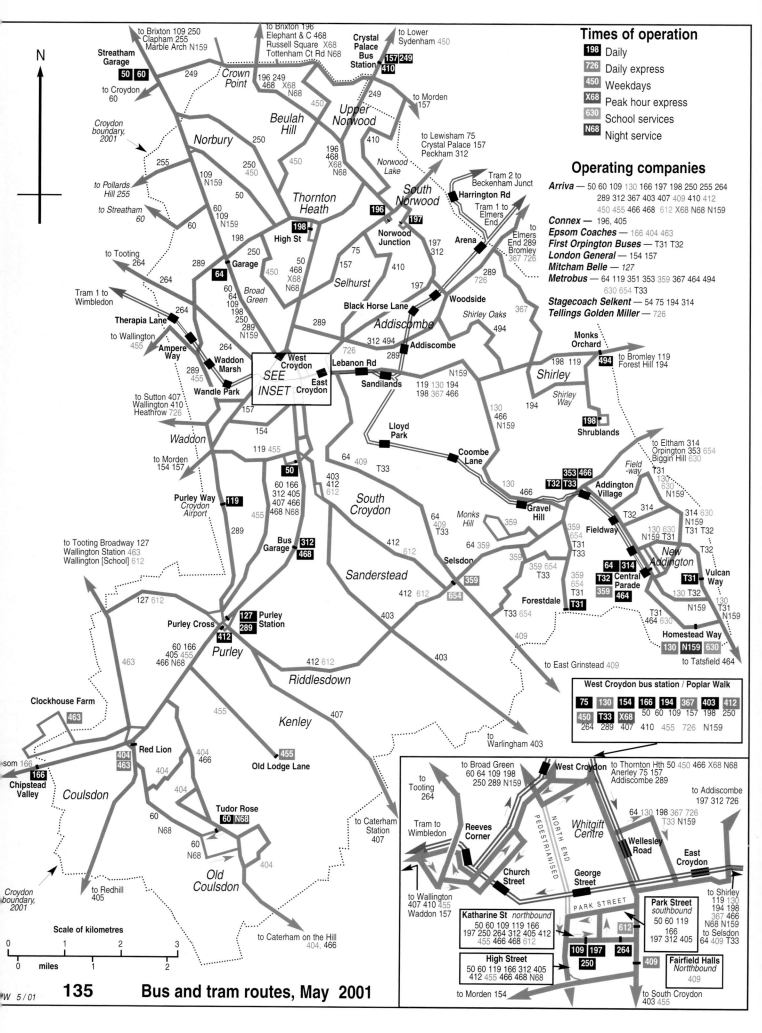

136 Station Road, West Croydon - 1927
(above)
The General company ran motor bus services into London's countryside at weekends from about 1912. Once the East Surrey Traction Company started its network of longer distance bus routes from Croydon there were even more opportunities for local residents to enjoy bus rides into Surrey and Kent. Here crowds were waiting to board a route 416 bus on August Bank Holiday 1927.

137 Station Road, West Croydon about 1933
(centre left)
One of East Surrey's ST type buses has the new but short-lived General fleetname, soon to be replaced by London Transport.

138 New Addington about 1938 (below left)
The First National Housing Trust built the first houses at New Addington on an isolated downland site five miles from Croydon. At first there was no public transport but from March 1938 a special bus service was put on to link the estate with the terminus of route 64 at Featherbed Lane. It was run by A. Bennett & Sons Shirley Coaches as seen here. The fare was 2d and it operated until 4th July 1939, when London Transport introduced its direct route 130 from Croydon running about every 20 to 30 minutes.

139 Croydon High Street about 1936
(above right)
By the mid 1930s buses were becoming more comfortable. In this postcard view one of London Transport's LT type buses is going south in the High Street on route 68 with other buses in the background.

140 A Wartime Loan - 1940 (centre right)
Early in the Second World War some provincial buses were loaned to London Transport to cover alleged shortages caused by bomb damage. Here a Portsmouth Corporation Tilling Stevens bus on route 12 is waiting to leave the forecourt of the *Red Deer*.

141 A Post-War Loan (below)
After the Second World War London Transport was again experiencing shortages of vehicles due to many buses being well past their intended life and prone to break down. In 1948 nearly 200 brand new Bristols built for companies across the country were sent to help out for up to a year. Here a green Bristol, intended for Crosville Motor Services, is on the route 68 bus stand in Junction Road, near the *Earl of Eldon* public house. The same route also saw green Eastern National and red United and Eastern Counties vehicles.

142 West Croydon - 15th April 1949
  (below right)
The pleasures of a ride into the country by bus continued to attract large crowds in the early post-war years. Here queues were waiting to board one of London Transport's green front entrance STL's in St Michael's Road. The 403 route was unusual as it crossed the highest point on the North Downs and had a special schedule for operation when snow made parts of the route impassable!

143 Thornton Heath Bus Garage - 7th July 1971 (left)

This site was first used as a horse tram depot in 1879, and for electric trams from 1901 to the end of 1949. The buildings were then demolished and a new bus garage was built. This opened on 8th April 1951 housing buses to replace the trams withdrawn the previous night. The site is thought to have been in use for public road transport purposes longer than any other in the London area. On this July day a number of the famous post-war AEC RT type buses were standing in the sun.

144 Addington Village Road - 16th October 1965 (centre left)

London Transport's famous new RM type Routemaster buses were introduced from the end of the 1950s, and in Croydon from 1960. Here one was on its way from New Addington to Croydon in the days before Addington Village Road was widened into the dual-carriageway Kent Gate Way. Trams now run on the central reservation where the hedge on the right once grew.

145 North Downs AEC Reliance Bus in Altyre Road - 1976 (above)

This was one of the first independent operators to run in the area. London Transport was very short of staff at the time and unable to provide a service to the new houses at Forestdale. This small operator was the forerunner of Metrobus whose blue buses now run on several routes in this area and further afield.

146 West Croydon Bus Station - 7th July 1973 (left)

This bus station was opened in 1963, largely on the site of the bombed Free Christian Church. It was improved and rebuilt with better facilities in 1984. In 1970 London Country Bus Services Ltd., part of the National Bus Company, had been formed to operate the country bus services in the area. One of their AN type Leyland Atlanteans was on route 470, and one of London Transport's DMS type Daimler Fleetlines was on express route C4. One person operation was by this time leading to the gradual phasing out of the conductors.

147 Bus in Katharine Street -
   5th August 1996 (right)
Privatisation led to London Country's local
operations being renamed 'London & Country'
in 1989 with an attractive new livery illustrated
here by one of the company's AD type Dennis
Arrows on route 405. In 1997 the operations
were rebranded as Arriva and route 405 was
transferred to Connex buses in 2001.

148 Southend Bus at West Croydon - 1976
   (below)
London Transport again suffered a severe
vehicle shortage in the mid 1970s. To help out,
buses from Southend Transport, including this
Leyland PD3, were hired for route 190. Other
hirings in the area were blue buses from
Maidstone Corporation on route 403 and
yellow Bournemouth Corporation buses on
routes 408 and 470.

149 Bus in Davidson Road -
   16th September 1996 (centre right)
Tendering of London bus routes began in 1985
followed by full privatisation in 1994. One
advantage of this has been that the network of
routes has extended into more areas. Here a
Dennis DRL type bus is in Davidson Road,
previously unserved by bus. Compare the 1933
and 2001 route maps on pages 60 and 61.

150 Disabled Accessible Bus -
   13th May 2000 (below right)
All new buses have now to be accessible to
people in wheelchairs. One of the new DLA
type buses on route 468 is seen here in
Brighton Road, South Croydon.

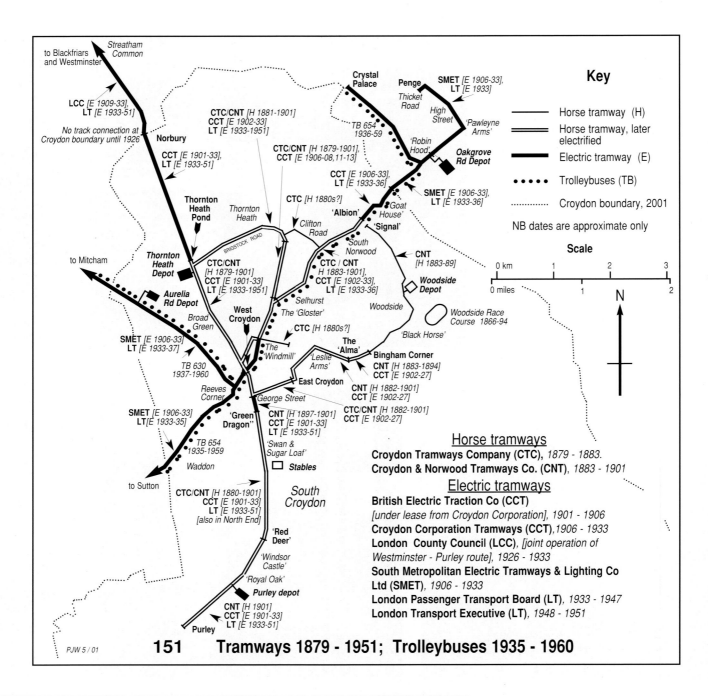

Key

— Horse tramway (H)

═ Horse tramway, later electrified

━ Electric tramway (E)

•••• Trolleybuses (TB)

⋯⋯ Croydon boundary, 2001

NB dates are approximate only

Scale

0 km ⟶ 1 ⟶ 2 ⟶ 3
0 miles ⟶ 1 ⟶ 2

N

to Blackfriars and Westminster

Streatham Common

LCC [E 1909-33], LT [E 1933-51]

No track connection at Croydon boundary until 1926

Norbury

CCT [E 1901-33], LT [E 1933-51]

Crystal Palace

Penge
Thicket Road
High Street

SMET [E 1906-33], LT [E 1933]

'Pawleyne Arms'

CTC/CNT [H 1881-1901] CCT [E 1902-33] LT [E 1933-1951]

CTC/CNT [H 1879-1901] CCT [E 1906-08,11-13]

TB 654 1936-59

'Robin Hood'

Oakgrove Rd Depot

SMET [E 1906-33], LT [E 1933-36]

CCT [E 1906-33], LT [E 1933-36]

CTC [H 1880s?]

Thornton Heath Pond

Thornton Heath

Thornton Heath Depot

BRIGSTOCK ROAD

Clifton Road

'Albion'

'Goat House'

'Signal'

South Norwood

CTC/CNT [H 1879-1901], CCT [E 1901-33] LT [E 1933-1951]

CTC / CNT H 1883-1901], CCT [E 1902-33], LT [E 1933-36]

CNT [H 1883-89]

Woodside Depot

to Mitcham

Aurelia Rd Depot

West Croydon

Broad Green

Selhurst

The 'Gloster'

Woodside

Woodside Race Course 1866-94

'Black Horse'

SMET [E 1906-33] LT [E 1933-37]

TB 630 1937-1960

CTC [H 1880s?]

'The Windmill'

The 'Alma'

'Leslie Arms'

Bingham Corner

CNT [H 1883-1894] CCT [E 1902-27]

Reeves Corner

George Street

East Croydon

CNT [H 1882-1901] CCT [E 1902-27]

SMET [E 1906-33] LT[E 1933-35]

'Green Dragon''

CNT [H 1897-1901] CCT [E 1901-33] LT [E 1933-51]

CTC/CNT [H 1882-1901] CCT [E 1902-27]

TB 654 1935-1959

'Swan & Sugar Loaf'

☐ Stables

Waddon

to Sutton

CTC/CNT [H 1880-1901] CCT [E 1901-33] LT [E 1933-51] [also in North End]

South Croydon

'Red Deer'

'Windsor Castle'

'Royal Oak'

Purley depot

CNT [H 1901] CCT [E 1901-33] LT [E 1933-51]

Purley

Horse tramways

Croydon Tramways Company (CTC), 1879 - 1883.
Croydon & Norwood Tramways Co. (CNT), 1883 - 1901

Electric tramways

British Electric Traction Co (CCT)
[under lease from Croydon Corporation], 1901 - 1906
Croydon Corporation Tramways (CCT), 1906 - 1933
London County Council (LCC), *[joint operation of Westminster - Purley route], 1926 - 1933*
South Metropolitan Electric Tramways & Lighting Co Ltd (SMET), 1906 - 1933
London Passenger Transport Board (LT), 1933 - 1947
London Transport Executive (LT), 1948 - 1951

PJW 5 / 01

151   Tramways 1879 - 1951; Trolleybuses 1935 - 1960

152 North End about 1885 (left)
A single-deck horse tram was outside the Whitgift Hospital as a double-deck horse tram passed Joshua Allders' shop. He was a director of the tramways company and it is recorded that one of his employees would from time to time leave the shop to check tickets on the trams. In 1890 the company had 14 trams and 95 horses.

154 Battery Tram - 1892 (right)
This battery electric tram was tried on the Thornton Heath - Crown Hill route for a few months in 1892 and was photographed at Thornton Heath Depot. The main problems were that the car emitted evil smelling fumes, and acid from the batteries was prone to spill and damage passenger's clothing, and probably the passengers! Other unsuccessful experiments with mechanical traction included a Connelly oil-engined car and a Luhrig gas-engined car, but horses continued in use until electrification from 1901 onwards.

Trams and Trolleybuses

Street tramways first appeared in New York in the 1830s. Early experiments in the 1860s in the United Kingdom did not work well and it was 1870 before the first successful horse tramway started running in London between Brixton and Kennington. Others soon followed, and in Croydon a group of local businessmen, headed by Joseph Spencer Balfour, and including Joshua Allder, formed a company to build some local routes. In 1878 the Croydon Tramways Bill received Royal Assent and the first section between Thornton Heath Pond and North End opened on 9th October 1879. Other routes soon followed but the extremely narrow High Street prevented lines being laid between George Street and Surrey Street, so an isolated route was built from Surrey Street (the *Green Dragon*) to the *Red Deer*.

In 1882 the Norwood & District Tramways Bill received Royal Assent and whilst the lines were under construction, the company set up under the Act amalgamated with the Croydon Tramways Company to form the Croydon & Norwood Tramways Company. Several of the new lines such as those along St James's Road, between Addiscombe, the Alma, and South Norwood, and along Clifton Road lasted for only a few years. There is a report that the Clifton Road route was operated by a single deck car "but the low boys used to throw stones at it from the clay pit". The pit became the site of Selhurst Park football ground.

The main advantage of tramways was that a horse could pull a much greater weight more smoothly on rails than on the poor road surfaces of the day. The tramway companies had to maintain the roadway between the rails and for 18 inches on either side, as well as paying rates to the local authority. This brought a considerable improvement to the road surfaces and benefited all road users, but was a burden to the companies.

By the mid-1890s Croydon's tramways were in a somewhat run down state. The Corporation had opened its first electric power station in 1896, with some electric street lighting being provided at the same time. By then electric tramways were opening in various parts of the United Kingdom. Croydon Corporation purchased the local tramways and obtained powers for their reconstruction and electrification. The tramways were leased to the British Electric Traction Company and the first line between the borough boundary at Norbury and at Purley was formally opened on 26th September 1901. Other lines to Thornton Heath, South Norwood and Addiscombe soon followed.

In 1906 the South Metropolitan Tramways and Lighting Company, a subsidiary of the British Electric Traction Company, opened routes from the borough boundary at Selby Road to Crystal Palace and Penge; and from West Croydon to Mitcham and Tooting, and to Sutton. Strained relations between the BET company and the Corporation led to the termination of the company's lease of the Corporation's tramways. For about a year the South Metropolitan trams ran from Crystal Palace and Penge only as far as the borough boundary at Selby Road. More satisfactory arrangements were soon reached whereby the Corporation trams ran outside the borough to Penge, and the South Metropolitan trams ran from Crystal Palace through to West Croydon. Meanwhile the separate lines from West Croydon to Sutton and Mitcham/Tooting were operated by the South Metropolitan company from the outset.

As motor vehicles became more reliable and more comfortable, so competition increased, particularly from buses. In 1931 a Royal Commission on Transport recommended that no new tramways should be built, and those existing should be gradually phased out. This was largely because it was felt trams obstructed other traffic, but the danger of boarding and alighting in the middle of the road was no doubt a major factor, as was the growing motoring lobby. Meanwhile trolleybuses were being introduced in many places. These took power from overhead wires but were not confined to rails and could pick up and set down passengers at the roadside. The London Passenger Transport Board was formed in 1933 and took over all local bus and tram routes. It soon started a programme of converting tram routes to trolleybus operation. The local tram routes to Sutton, Crystal Palace and Mitcham were converted to trolleybuses by 1937, but the war halted further changes. After the war it was decided to replace the remaining trams by motor buses and Croydon's last tram ran in 1951. The trolleybuses, too, were replaced by motor buses in 1959/60. Nearly sixty years of electric traction on local roads had ended and few people then foresaw that trams would one day return.

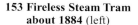

153 Fireless Steam Tram about 1884 (left)
The Croydon & Norwood Tramways Company was interested in mechanical traction and in 1884 ordered six fireless steam trams from the Hohenzollern Company in Dusseldorf. The tram locomotives, which would have been fuelled with compressed steam at the depot, pulled a separate passenger vehicle. They were apparently delivered to the depot at Spring Lane, Woodside and worked on trial but from reports in the local press, do not seem to have been used in passenger service. They are thought to have been returned to the manufacturers as unsatisfactory.

155 Broad Green about 1906 (above)
The illustrations on these two pages are all Edwardian postcards. They give a good impression of the tramway liveries in use early in the twentieth century. Here one of the Croydon Corporation's bogie tramcars is on its way to Purley, with St James's Road on the left. There was no protection for the motorman on these cars. The livery at the time was Munich Lake (really chocolate) and white.

156 Swan and Sugar Loaf about 1906 (below)
A Croydon Corporation four-wheeled tramcar was about to pass the public house which had been rebuilt in 1896. In 2001 this scene had changed very little, although the Methodist Church on the right was demolished in the 1980s, and the trams had gone in 1951.

157 George Street about 1906 (above)
A Corporation four-wheeled tramcar was passing Dingwall Road on single track before the passing loop at East Croydon Station. The longer eight-wheeled bogie trams could not be used on the routes to Addiscombe or South Norwood because of the single track sections with short passing loops. The clock tower on the right was part of Thrift's Grocery Warehouse, and with nearly all the other buildings in this view was demolished for road widening in the 1960s. Tramlink's westbound track now follows approximately the same alignment as the track seen here.

158 Addiscombe Terminus about 1904
    (below left)
The rural nature of this spot is evident but within a few years the trams had encouraged housing development in the area. The railway bridge carried the Woodside and South Croydon line across Lower Addiscombe Road.

Tramlink now runs on the same alignment, but at street level. Bingham Road is on the right and a railway halt was opened there in 1906. See illustrations 82 and 83 on page 39 for later views in Bingham Road.

159 Croydon Road, Anerley about 1906
    (below right)
This photograph shows one of the South Metropolitan Electric Tramways and Lighting Company's tramcars in the attractive green and white livery of early years. From the opening of the Penge and Crystal Palace lines in 1906 the company's trams terminated at the Croydon borough boundary at Selby Road. When agreement was reached with Croydon Corporation, through running started on 24th June 1907. This photograph was taken in the Penge Urban District Council area near the temporary Selby Road terminus.

160 Brighton Road, Purley - Summer 1901
(left)
One of the new electric tramcars was on test near Purley Tram Depot. The 'Providence' lifeguards originally fitted were clumsy and were soon replaced with a more conventional type. In the background is one of the horse-trams that provided a service over the new tracks south of the *Red Deer* from May 1901 until electric trams started carrying passengers later in the year.

Croydon Corporation Tramways Band.

161 Croydon Corporation Tramways Band about 1909 (centre left)
On this postcard sent to friends late in 1909, the writer says "I am sending you a postcard of the Croydon Crawlers". Most transport operators had sports and social activities for their workers in the days when people had to make their own entertainment and had much less choice of leisure activities than today. Mr Thomas Goodyer, the tramways manager is seated next to the bandmaster.

162 Near Thornton Heath Pond about 1906
(below)
The Croydon Corporation Tramway Offices were in Brigstock Villa, on the right. The main depot and workshops were behind. The works tram was just entering the narrow entrance to the depot, while a bogie tramcar bound for Thornton Heath High Street was turning into Brigstock Road. The splendid wagonette had perhaps proved just too irresistible for the young lad who appears to be having a joy-ride.

63 Purley - 1907 (right)
This was the gateway to attractive downland countryside. In the days when very few people had holidays, cars, or for that matter much money, a day out in the country could be had for a few pence. The crowd queuing for trams at Purley on Easter Monday 1907 had no worries about blocking half the width of the Brighton Road, Russell Hill Road and Banstead Road on the right, and the main Eastbourne Road on the left! Even on a bank holiday in those days road traffic was very light.

164 Norbury Tram Terminus - 1919
(centre right)
The Corporation's trams reached the extremities of the borough at Purley and Norbury. From 1909 the London County Council trams were extended from Streatham to Norbury but a short gap in the track separated the two systems until 1926. One of the London County Council's E/1 class trams was facing a Corporation four-wheeler at the Hermitage Bridge terminus on a sunny afternoon just after the First World War. The 'P' stencil on the headlight was a wartime means of showing the destination (Purley) in the blackout.

165 Tram in Oakfield Road -
1st August 1925 (below left)
Oakfield Road was used by trams coming into Croydon from Norwood until 1926. They then ran into London Road and Station Road, leaving via Wellesley Road to Spurgeon's Bridge. Here a South Metropolitan tramcar was on its way to West Croydon. The driver had already changed the destination indicator to Crystal Palace. From 1926 trams used Wellesley Road both ways but Oakfield Road was used by buses coming into Croydon until the bus station opened in the 1960s.

166 Trams in Whitehorse Road about 1912
(below right)
The part of Whitehorse Road between Whitehorse Lane and the Gloster public house was used by horse trams for a while, and electric trams were introduced in 1906. However the route never seemed to attract many passengers and it was closed in 1908. The Corporation reopened it in 1911, but it was again closed in 1913 and did not reopen after this.

167 Anerley Hill - 1906 (left)
The tramway from the *Robin Hood*, Anerley to the bottom of Anerley Hill opened on 12th April 1906. This photograph must have been taken about this time as the northbound track was blocked by a contractor's hut. The steep section up the hill could not be opened until the South Metropolitan company had persuaded sufficient drivers with at least six years' experience to transfer from other undertakings. Special brakes had to be provided on the trams used on the hill, which was the steepest tram route in the whole of the London area. The section up the hill opened on 28th May 1906.

The Crystal Palace attracted a lot of traffic for the trams and it dominated the area from its removal from Hyde Park in 1854 until destroyed by fire in 1936. Shortly before, trolleybuses had replaced the trams on this route.

168 Trams at West Croydon - about 1930
    (above right)
The South Metropolitan company built two lines on the west of Croydon, to Sutton and to Tooting. Both routes started at the top of Tamworth Road before splitting at Lower Church Street. They ran through quite a lot of open country after leaving the town and had much of the character of interurban lines. Pleasure riders were attracted by advertisements such as 'Fresh Air Rides across Breezy Mitcham Common and to Sutton'!

169 Tramway Parcels Express (centre right)
The South Metropolitan Electric Tramways operated a parcels service from June 1908. A contemporary trade journal said, "The S.M.E.T. made a new departure on Tuesday by inaugurating a Tramway Parcels express, in connection with the service of cars between Tooting and Croydon, Wallington, Carshalton and Mitcham. Conductors receive packages at any of the recognised stopping places, or they may be left at certain agents and they are dealt with by special messengers in uniform. The rates for collection and delivery within half a mile of any part of the lines vary between 7lb. for 3d. and 56lb. for 7d." This tram was at the corner of Church Street and Ellis David Place, parcels baskets were on the front platform and several of the uniformed messengers were in attendance. The parcels service was discontinued at the end of 1911.

170 Tamworth Road/Lower Church Street
    about 1932 (below right)
In 1931 the South Metropolitan company borrowed ten covered top London United Tramways cars from the Kingston area for use mainly on the Mitcham route. One was here turning into Lower Church Street from Tamworth Road. This was a difficult junction which was controlled by signals. Trams coming from the Mitcham direction had to come on to the wrong track in Tamworth Road and then over the facing crossover just visible in the foreground, to gain the left hand track. (see also illustration 176 on page 75).

171 Brigstock Road about 1936
In 1928 the Corporation fitted top-deck covers to their ten 1902 bogie cars as seen here. These vehicles continued in service with London Transport until replaced by more modern vehicles withdrawn from north London between 1936 and 1937. Even in the 1930s some tram drivers had virtually no protection from the elements. Old tramwaymen told of cold snowy days when their moustaches froze and icicles formed by the time they reached the terminus!

172 Station Road, West Croydon in 1935
The Sutton tram route was converted to trolleybus operation on 8th December 1935. Here one of the new vehicles was alongside an open-top tram still running on the Crystal Palace route. These were the last such still in regular service in the London area. They too were replaced by trolleybuses on 9th February 1936.

173 Clearance Test - High Street about 1938
In 1937/38 one hundred modern 'Feltham' type tramcars were displaced by trolleybus conversion schemes in north London. They were transferred to south London and many worked on routes 16 and 18 from Purley to the Victoria Embankment. This is thought to be an official photograph demonstrating that there was insufficient space for a Feltham tramcar to overtake a Green Line coach outside the Head Post Office.

**174 E/1 Class Tramcar - Lower Saloon
about 1950** (above right)
The driver and conductor pose for the photographer in car 394. This was one of 25 new cars bought by Croydon Corporation in 1927 and 1928 for the joint London County Council/Corporation through Purley/Embankment service. They remained at Thornton Heath Depot until Croydon's trams were replaced by buses in 1951, and most saw further service from other depots for some months before being scrapped.

**175 E/1 Class Tramcar - Upper Saloon
about 1950** (centre right)
A view on the upper deck of the same tramcar. Single and double seats were provided downstairs where the body was slightly narrower and standing was allowed. There were double seats on both sides of the gangway upstairs.

**176 Lower Church Street -
10th January 1959** (below right)
This photograph shows the tight corner which the trams had to negotiate when turning into Tamworth Road from Lower Church Street (see illustration 170 on page 73). The Mitcham tram route was in 1933 replaced by an extension of the former LCC route 30 from Harlesden to Mitcham on to West Croydon. Trolleybus route 630 replaced the trams on 12th September 1937 and had similar problems to the trams in negotiating this junction, signals still being needed. On the left was the former Market Hall which was at one time used by the South Metropolitan Company as offices and a waiting room. All the buildings seen here were demolished in the 1970s and trams again pass the spot which has changed out of all recognition. See plan, illustration 201 on page 85.

177 North End - 1st September 1945
(above left)
Harold Bennett, a professional photographer
took the photograph below before going to
have tea in Wilson's Café. He then took this
general view from an upstairs window. Note
the *Scala* Cinema on the right which had been
incorporated in Allders' store, and how few
cars were around.

178 Whitgift Hospital - 1st September 1945
(below left)
Photographed a couple of weeks after VJ (Victory
over Japan) Day, the flags were still flying to
celebrate the event. An STL type bus on route 68
was squeezing alongside an E/3 tram on local
service 42. The bus had several windows boarded
up following wartime damage, and the tram still
had its white painted fender from blackout days.

179 West Croydon - 28th February 1959 (above)
The cross roads at West Croydon viewed from an
upstairs window of the *Railway Bell* (by 2001
called the *Arkwright's Wheel*). A P1 class
trolleybus on route 630 is approaching the
terminus in Station Road and one of the short B1
class vehicles is on its way to Sutton on route 654.

180 Tamworth Road about 1959 (centre right)
A 630 trolleybus has just left the stop at the top of
Tamworth Road, and another trolleybus is
overtaking a green RT on route 408.

181 Mitcham Common about 1959 (right)
Mitcham Common provided plenty of opportunity
for fast journeys on trolleybus route 630. This
view shows one speeding past having just crossed
Beddington Lane on its way to Harlesden.

182 Brigstock Road about 1950 (above)
Photographed from a Thornton Heath bound tram, an E/3 class tram on its way to Croydon was about to enter the passing loop near the Fire Station. There was still a vacant bomb site on the left, but Trumble Gardens had been formed on the right-hand bomb site. Coal lorries were a familiar sight until smokeless zones were introduced. Otherwise there was only a horse-drawn milk float and one car visible. Grange Wood on the hill in the distance is a remnant of the Great North Wood which was once a formidable barrier between Croydon and London.

**183 London Road, Norbury -
13th August 1949** (below)
Looking north near Pollards Hill, a Feltham class tram was on its way to Purley. A track repair gang was busy on the northbound track, their equipment taking power from the overhead wires.

184 Purley Tram Depot - 1951 (right)
Purley Depot became a store in 1937. It was brought back into regular use at the beginning of 1950 so that Thornton Heath Depot could be demolished and a bus garage built on its site. This photograph was taken at the depot just before final closure in April 1951.

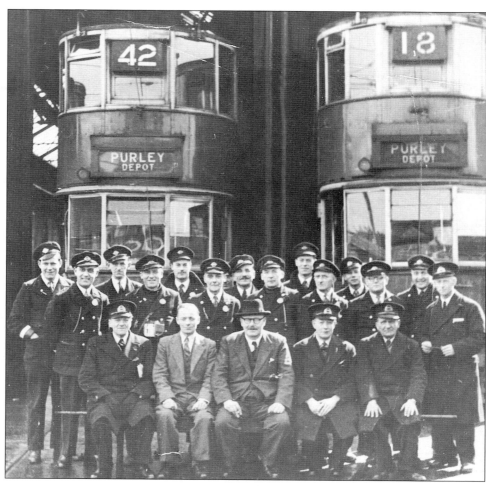

185 Last Tram - 7th April 1951 (below)
Trams were regarded with affection by many people. The last tram in Croydon left Purley Depot late in the evening and was followed to Thornton Heath Pond by hooting motor cars, and waved off by cheering crowds. In this photograph it was turning from London Road into Brigstock Road at the end of its journey where anything removable, including some of the seats, was taken away as a souvenir. It had been hired by the Infantile Paralysis Fellowship and tickets were sold at 5/- each to raise funds. The Mayor, Alderman Maurice Stacey, and Fred Harris, MP for North Croydon drove the tram for part of the way.

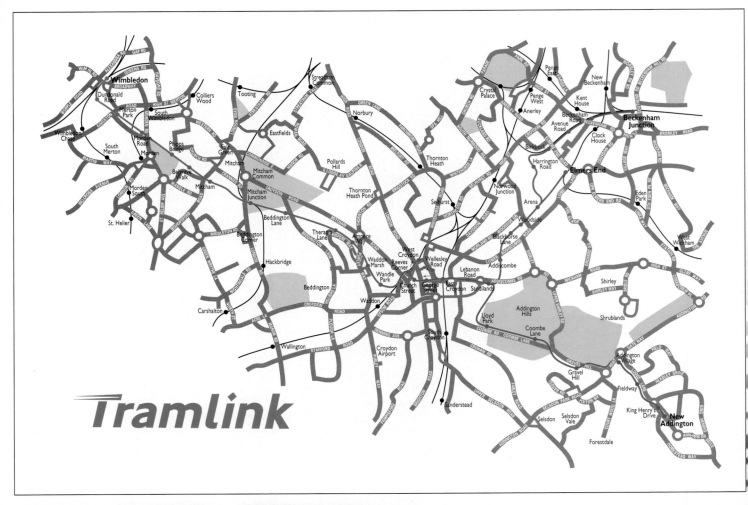

Croydon Tramlink

186 Tramlink Map (above left)

187 Laying the First Rails - 25th June 1998
(below, far left)
Diversion of underground cables and water mains started in early 1997, but it was not until mid-1998 that signs of real progress became obvious. The first tram rails to be put in place were in Addiscombe Road near the corner of Park Hill Road. One rail had been placed in its concrete groove, and preparations were being made to place the opposite rail in position.

188 Crown Hill - 24th May 1999 (below left)
The height of the overhead wire had to be carefully checked as seen here.

189 Welding the lines - 1906 (below)
and **190 21st January 1999** (below right)
The left-hand picture is taken from a postcard showing work on the South Metropolitan Electric Tramways in Wallington. The right-hand picture shows thermit welding of the track on the corner of Wellesley Road and George Street 93 years later. The technique has changed very little.

Croydon grew rapidly in importance as a commercial centre from the 1960s. Major redevelopment schemes brought a large number of office blocks, new shopping centres and increasing problems of traffic congestion. Meanwhile in the mid 1970s schemes for an automatic people mover to link the town with New Addington came to nothing but the problems of providing good transport for this isolated township remained.

By the 1980s trams and light railways were making a comeback in cities in various parts of the world, including the USA. It was found that while few motorists were prepared to forsake their cars for buses, light rail could attract motorists. There were environmental benefits too. In 1986 London Transport and British Rail published a report *Light Rail for London?* This identified some lightly used railway lines that might usefully be extended and converted to light railways/tramways. A small network in the Croydon area seemed promising and further studies led to the Croydon Tramlink Act which received Royal Assent on 21st July 1994.

The project involved conversion of the West Croydon to Wimbledon railway to tramway operation, with extra stops. Leaving the rail alignment at Wandle Park, a new flyover now takes the trams over the Croydon/Epsom railway line and on to the street to run up Tamworth Road, past West Croydon Station, along Wellesley Road and George Street to East Croydon Station. In the other direction trams go down George Street, Crown Hill and Church

Street, then either continue to Wimbledon, or return via Tamworth Road. From East Croydon trams run along Addiscombe Road to Sandilands where they join the trackbed of the disused Woodside and South Croydon railway line, closed in 1983. The routes split here, one going south and leaving the former railway alignment at Coombe Road, then running through fields and woods and alongside roads to New Addington. The other routes turn north along the former railway alignment to about half a mile east of Woodside. One line then continues the short distance to Elmers End, whilst the other crosses South Norwood Country Park to join and run alongside the existing railway line to Birkbeck and Beckenham Junction. The railway line between Addiscombe and Elmers End closed in 1997 to accommodate the tramway.

There was vocal opposition to the scheme but after the Parliamentary Bill became an Act and a Consortium was selected to take the project forward, Croydon saw the biggest civil engineering works in the area since railways first appeared in the 1830s. Tramlink opened in stages over several weeks from 10th May 2000 and is proving very successful. The aims of the Victorian entrepreneurs who built the Wimbledon branch in 1855, the Mid-Kent line to Addiscombe in 1864, and the Woodside and South Croydon Railway in 1884 may not have been realised at the time but their lines are now proving much more useful and carrying far more passengers than ever before!

191 George Street - 6th August 1927
(above left) and
192 - 1st December 1998 (centre left)
The top view shows the Addiscombe tram track being removed in 1927. Below is the view from a similar position 71 years later. It shows the concrete base for the new tram track almost ready to receive the rails. Most of the buildings remain and the street is still recognisable.

193 Oaks Road, Shirley - 14th July 1999
Looking west from Addington Hills these two road-rail vehicles which could run on both roads and railway tracks were used for the installation of the overhead wires for the new tramway.

194 Gauging Test - 1st June 1999
This new bridge was built to take trams from the former Wimbledon branch railway line across the Croydon/Sutton railway line and into the town centre streets. The first tram was being towed across the bridge by a road-rail lorry in the afternoon, ready to be towed around the town later that night to test clearances.

195 First Tram Under Power -
16th June 1999
Two weeks after the gauging run, the first tram to run into the town under power arrived at Cairo New Road early in the morning. It is seen here passing the almshouses and about to descend Crown Hill on its first test run. A police escort was provided and a number of contractor's staff and interested spectators were watching proceedings.

196 New Addington - 6th May 2000
The trams are painted in traditional London red and white livery and are numbered to follow on from the highest number in the original London Transport fleet. Tram 2536 was approaching the King Henry's Drive stop a few days before public service started on 10th May. The Beckenham branch opened shortly afterwards on 23rd May and the Wimbledon/Elmers End route completed the system on 30th May 2000.

197 Woodside Station - July 1990
A two car EPB unit in Network South East livery was photographed on the Elmers End to Addiscombe shuttle service a few years before the new Networker trains came into use on the branch.

198 Woodside Tram Stop - 10th June 2000
The Addiscombe - Elmers End railway line having closed at the end of May 1997, the track needed for Tramlink was refurbished and the platforms and canopies at Woodside were removed. The new tram stop is typical of those throughout the system with low platforms and simple shelters. The old station building may be used for other purposes but in 2001 was boarded up.

199 East Croydon Station - 8th May 2001
A three track tram stop has been built immediately outside the modern steel and glass station. There is a new small bus station just to the east of this.

200 En Route to New Addington - 11th May 2000

Once this route leaves the former railway tunnels and alignment between Sandilands and Coombe Road it turns sharply to the east and runs along the edge of Lloyd Park. It then goes through the grounds of Geoffrey Harris House, crossing the access roadway and past the lodge seen here. It continues through the woodland of Addington Hills and then past fields on what must be one of the most attractive tram routes in Britain. Tram 2550, one of five in an overall advertising livery, promotes First Group, the operators of the system.

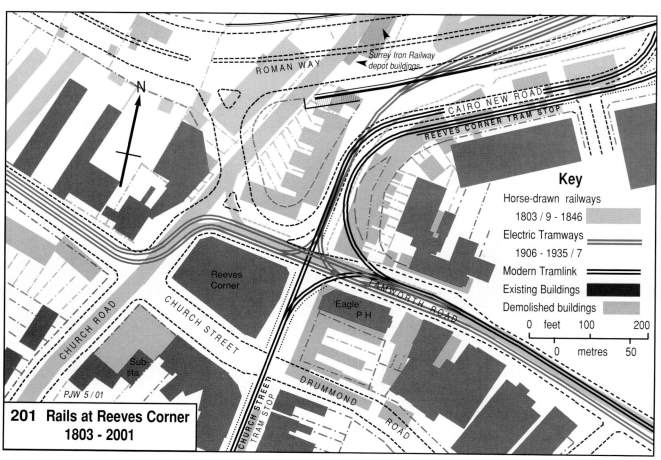

Key

Horse-drawn railways
1803 / 9 - 1846

Electric Tramways
1906 - 1935 / 7

Modern Tramlink

Existing Buildings

Demolished buildings

0 feet 100 200

0 metres 50

PJW 5 / 01

201 Rails at Reeves Corner
1803 - 2001

202 Airship in Croydon - 1st May 1908 (left)
Henry Spencer intended to fly from
Wandsworth to St Paul's, but a strong wind
blew him off course and he landed at 5.0 pm in
a large field in Bute Road, near the
Corporation electricity works. The *Croydon
Advertiser* reported that great excitement had
been caused on the Friday evening, especially
in the neighbourhood of Mitcham Road when
the airship landed.

**203 Aeroplane at Waddon - Saturday 6th
May 1911** (centre left)
Clarence Greswell, flying a 50 hp Bleriot from
Hendon to Brooklands, lost his way in mist
and landed in a field at Waddon, near the
Borough Isolation Hospital. He had to await
the arrival of a mechanic from Hendon before
he could take off and crowds of interested
spectators went to the scene. For many it was
the first aircraft they had seen.

**204 Grahame White at Crystal Palace - 7th
July 1910** (below)
The *Croydon Advertiser* reported that "Mr
Grahame White's attempted flight from Crystal
Palace to Bournemouth ended in failure at
South Norwood Hill......He got away from the
Palace Grounds at 2.25pm and swung round to
the south west.......His motor was not working
satisfactorily, this adding to the danger of the
situation and he decided to drop into the
sloping field which lies between Howden Road
and Woodvale Avenue". Large crowds
assembled, broke through the fence, and
carried away some fragments from the
damaged machine as mementoes.

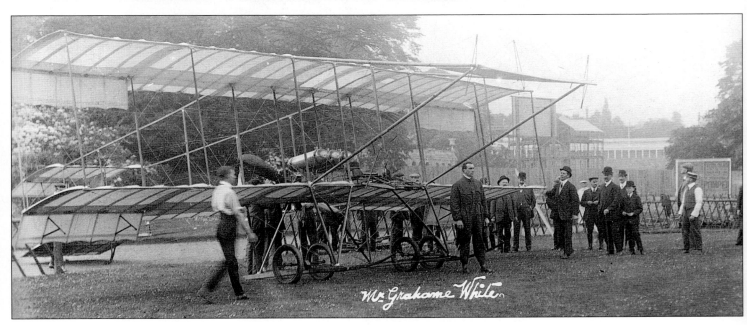

Aeronautics and Aviation

The first manned balloon-ascent in the world took place in Paris in 1783. Two years later, the first ascent in Surrey took place at Molesey. Over the ensuing years there were many flights some of which may well have passed over Croydon. In 1839 the Beulah Spa at Upper Norwood advertised that, in honour of the opening of the London and Croydon Railway, Mr J.W. Hoar would make a grand ascent from the gardens in his new Montgolfier Balloon of enormous proportions. This event was a total failure but balloon ascents and displays frequently featured at the Beulah Spa Gardens. It was in 1859 that the first of many balloon-ascents started from the Crystal Palace. The Aeronautical Society of Great Britain was formed in 1866, and held the first Aeronautical Exhibition at Crystal Palace in 1868.

205 Aviator Robert Slack at Coulsdon - 1912
Robert Slack was engaged by the International Correspondence Schools to make an aerial tour of 300 miles in a Bleriot machine. He started by flying from Hendon aerodrome to a field at the top of Smitham Downs Road where this photograph was taken. On the following day some 2,000 people watched him make a local flight in aid of Croydon General Hospital. The collection raised £20. This postcard included the message that 'this aviator was here for a week. We saw some splendid flights'.

By the start of the twentieth century, powered airships were starting to appear and the first cross-country flight from Crystal Palace to Eastcote in Middlesex took place on 22nd September 1902. The first sustained flight by an aircraft in Britain took place at South Farnborough, Hampshire on 19th October 1908 when Samuel Cody flew 1,390 feet in a biplane of his own design and construction.

In December 1915 the Royal Flying Corps (later to become the Royal Air Force) established an aerodrome at Beddington, south of Stafford Road, and west of Plough Lane two miles west of Croydon. This was part of the air defence of London and planes took off on a number of occasions to attack raiding Zeppelins. During 1918 National Aircraft Factory Number One was built on an adjoining site, to the east of Plough Lane and next to Coldharbour Lane (now Purley Way). A test aerodrome, Waddon, was laid out alongside. Meanwhile another aerodrome was brought into use at Kenley in March 1917 and this became a Royal Air Force fighter station from 1918 until 1965. It played a very important part in the Battle of Britain in 1940 and at the beginning of the present century is used by gliders.

From Sunday 28th March 1920 the two former military airfields at Beddington and Waddon were combined to form 'The Official Air Terminus for London'. They were linked by means of an aircraft level crossing over Plough Lane. The Royal Flying Corps huts at Plough Lane formed the terminal buildings until 30th January 1928 when the new purpose-built terminal buildings on the recently opened Purley Way were ready.

From 1920 to 1939 Croydon Airport was the world's most important centre of air transport services. Many of the great events in aviation history took place there with the inauguration of new air routes and record-breaking flights. During the Second World War it was used by the Royal Air Force and, with Kenley and nearby Biggin Hill, played an important part in the Battle of Britain. Returning to civil use in 1946 it was too small for the larger aircraft then on the drawing board and it closed on 30th September 1959, services being moved to Gatwick.

Two other small local airfields should be mentioned. The British Air Transport Company moved about eight aircraft to a field at Addington around 1930. This proved to be unsatisfactory and the company moved to Gatwick in 1933. Two years later, in 1935, a small private aerodrome was established by Mr Charles Gardner at Hamsey Green between Warlingham and Sanderstead. Not surprisingly it closed in 1939 but was used for training purposes for a while afterwards.

206 Kenley Aerodrome about 1927
(above left)
In 1917 the Royal Flying Corps appropriated 81 acres of common land at Kenley under the Defence of the Realm Act. It was to be used as part of the Air Defence of London and subsequently remained in use by the Royal Air Force until 1965. The airfield played an important part in the Second World War, and particularly the 1940 Battle of Britain. At the beginning of the twenty first century part has been returned to common land but some remains in use as a gliding school. This view shows Gloster Gamecocks of Squadron Number 23 which was based at Kenley from 1927 until 1932.

207 Croydon Aerodrome Entrance about 1921 (centre left)
The aerodrome had been in civil use for a very short time when this photograph was taken. It has been described as "resembling a wild-west township in early days" and the former Royal Flying Corps buildings seen here remained in use until the new airport was opened in 1928 further to the east on Purley Way. All the airlines advertising here were merged into Imperial Airways in 1924.

208 Croydon Aerodrome about 1921 (below)
Another view of the first airport, with an AVRO 548 which had three separate cockpits, one for the pilot and two for passengers. The control tower and customs shed are in the background.

Notes for Comfort and Convenience of Passengers.

Special clothing is not necessary for air travel; clothing suitable for a motor-car journey is adequate.

Maps of routes can be obtained free at the various stations before departure.

Do not be concerned if the machine on starting taxies slowly towards a corner of the aerodrome. An aeroplane always starts and lands head against the wind. After a small run the machine almost imperceptibly rises from the ground.

We recommend passengers to place cotton wool in their ears to deaden the noise caused by the engines.

Slight deafness is sometimes caused by atmospheric pressure, and *immediate* relief can be obtained by either just blowing your nose, with the nostrils pinched together, or, when landing, by going through the action of swallowing.

In order to turn, an aeroplane banks—one side is raised above the horizontal and the other side lowered. This is a perfectly safe movement.

"Air pockets" do not exist, and when "bumps" occur they are caused by upward and downward currents of air, which have a similar effect upon aeroplanes as waves have on ships.

Dizziness, as experienced by some people when looking down from a high building, is unknown in aeroplanes, as there is no connection with the earth.

Air sickness affects fewer passengers than sea sickness; several of the proprietary remedies are completely efficacious. Cuspidors are provided for the use of passengers. Experienced passengers say that the finest cure for sea sickness is fresh air.

The windows of the cabin can be opened or shut as desired.

All Imperial machines flying on the Continental scheduled services have lavatory accommodation at the rear of the cabin, and passengers can freely move about the cabin without affecting the balance of the aeroplane.

Drinking water and glasses are carried on all Imperial aeroplanes.

It is prohibited by Government Regulations to smoke or light matches in the aeroplanes.

Nothing whatsoever should be thrown out of the windows of the aeroplane.

In the case of necessity, passengers can communicate with the pilot through the aperture in front of the cabin.

Your pilot is in constant touch with his Terminal Aerodrome by means of wireless telephony. He receives reports regarding the weather conditions at frequent intervals, and can ask for any information he needs at any time.

209 Notes for Passengers (left)
Flying must have seemed quite an adventure in the early days. These notes provided guidance for intending passengers.

210 Aircraft Interior about 1923 (above)
The accommodation in early civil aircraft can best be described as spartan. This is thought to be the interior of a W10 Hamilton or an Argosy 2.

**211 Arrival of Alan Cobham -
13th March 1926** (below)
Alan Cobham, probably the most famous British airman at the time, flew to Cape Town and back in 1925/6. The journey took five months, flying from airfield to airfield around the world. His small aircraft is just visible to the right of the large Handley Page W 8. The huge crowd that spilled on to the airfield to greet him after his epic flight was typical of the welcome accorded to aviators of the day and scenes such as this occurred at Croydon on many occasions.

212 The R 33 Airship at Croydon - 1921 (above)

Airships were expected to be the air transport of the future but various problems meant that initial expectations were not fulfilled. This mooring mast was provided specially for the R33 but it was moored there only once; the mast was demolished in the same year.

213 The New Airport (left)

Horatius, one of the famous Handley Page HP42 aircraft was photographed as it flew over the new control tower and terminal building in the early 1930s.

214 Advertising Leaflet

Surrey Flying Services was based at Croydon Airport and operated pleasure flights as well as taking aerial photographs of many places throughout the country.

215 Main Booking Hall about 1935
This was the equivalent of one of the terminals at Heathrow or Gatwick today. After the airport closed in 1959 the booking hall was used for various purposes but has now been restored to resemble its former appearance. It is used for various functions and as a reception area for offices in the former terminal building.

216 A Wartime Winter - Late January 1940
Civil flying ceased on the outbreak of war in 1939, and Croydon immediately became an important fighter station for the Royal Air Force. The 1940 winter was claimed to be the worst for 73 years and the airport was icebound for most of January. Here snow is being cleared from the airfield and a Blenheim, probably of 92 Squadron, is warming up its engines.

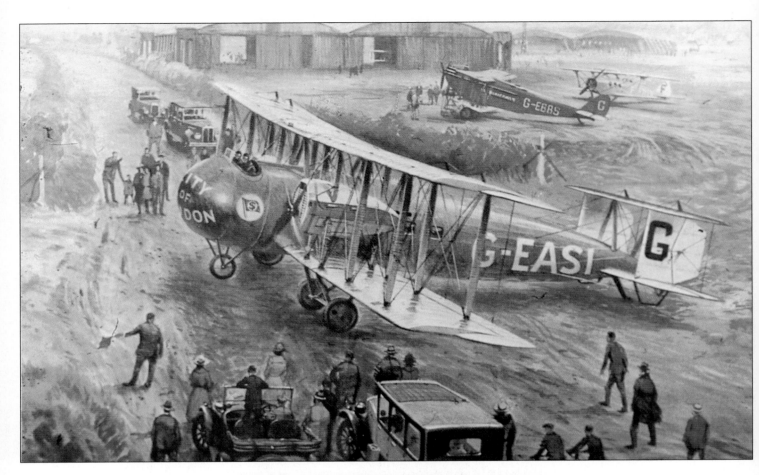

217 Plough Lane in the Early 1920s
(above)
This modern painting by Kenneth McDonough shows the aircraft level-crossing in Plough Lane, looking south. Instone Air Line Vimy, City of London, is crossing from the west side ready to take-off.

218 Airport Guide (left)
This guide was published in 1930 and the cover gives a colourful impression of the famous airport.

219 Morton Air Services Timetable - 1959
This timetable leaflet is from the last year of Croydon Airport's use for civil aviation.

220 Air Show - 30th May 1988
Large crowds attended the air shows on the former airfield in 1980 and 1988 when for a brief time the great days of Croydon Airport were commemorated. Efforts to arrange further similar events have failed largely due to air traffic control problems.

221 Croydon Airport Heritage Centre - 2000
The old control tower has been converted into a small museum and was initially open on the first Sunday of each month. This view inside the control tower shows its restoration to almost original condition.

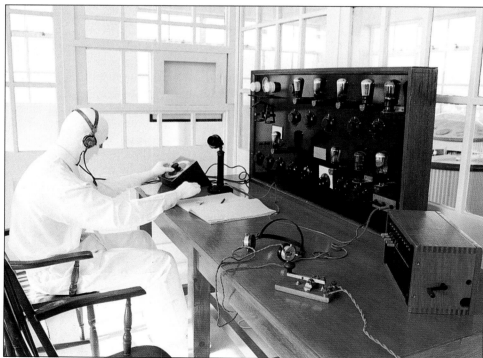

Transport improvements in the nineteenth and twentieth centuries brought great changes to the English landscape and to our way of life. The railway made it possible for workers to travel some distance from home to work, and to live in congenial surroundings. The tram and the motor bus provided convenient travel in towns and away from the railway stations. The motor car has given a much greater choice of home in relation to workplace. It has also brought problems of congestion and pollution combined with social changes. Few people now walk to the shops, meeting their neighbours on the way and finding time to chat. Many children are taken to and from school by car, lacking exercise and social contact. Vast areas of land have been covered in concrete to provide parking places. Where there are few garages suburban roads are lined with parked cars from end to end, causing obstruction to the highway which was intended for movement, not the storing of vehicles.

Bus services, especially in rural areas have been withdrawn, leaving people who do not have cars isolated. An examination of local road and rail timetables from the 1980s shows that Croydon has since lost long-standing direct bus links with towns such as Westerham, Sevenoaks, Tonbridge, Reigate, Dorking, Horsham, Epsom, Leatherhead, and Guildford. However, some improvements in direct train services have taken place with Thameslink services to north London, St Albans, Luton and Bedford, Connex services to Southampton and Bournemouth, and to Watford and Rugby, and a South West Trains service to Guildford.

The new Tramlink system has vastly improved east-west links around Croydon and transformed some local journeys which were previously very slow and difficult to make. The next few years may see some extensions but the great problem of congestion and pollution caused by motor vehicles is very difficult to resolve.

The car is comfortable and convenient but its use in towns will have to be controlled and possibly made much more expensive, with much greater enforcement of traffic regulations. Perhaps only when traffic offences are regarded as anti-social in the same way as drink and driving are, will attitudes change. But public transport will have to be improved and made much more reliable and pleasant. Tramlink is only the start.

Without the benefit of a crystal ball it is impossible to anticipate what the future may hold. A reader of this publication in fifty years time will have a much better idea. It is hoped too that he or she will also better understand some of the influences that made Croydon grow from a small market town into one of the largest commercial centres in the country in a matter of a little more than 130 years.

Bibliography

Baddeley, G.E. — *THE TRAMWAYS OF CROYDON (REVISED EDITION)*, The Light Rail Transit Association, 1983.

Bayliss, Derek A. — *RETRACING THE FIRST PUBLIC RAILWAY*. Living History Publications, 1981.

"Bell Street" — *EAST SURREY* H.J Publications, 1974.

Cluett, Douglas;Nash, Joanna and Learmonth, Bob — *CROYDON AIRPORT, THE GREAT DAYS, 1928-1939* Sutton Libraries and Arts Services, 1980.

Cluett, Douglas; Bogle, Joanna and Learmonth, Bob — *CROYDON AIRPORT, THE BATTLE FOR BRITAIN, 1939-40* Sutton Libraries and Arts Services, 1984.

Gent, John B. and Meredith, John H. — *CROYDON'S TRAMWAYS*, Middleton Press, 1999.

Gillham, John C. — *WIMBLEDON TO BECKENHAM BEFORE TRAMLINK*, Middleton Press, 2001.

King, J.T. and Newman, A.G — *SOUTHBOUND FROM CROYDON*. Omnibus Society and Bourne Society, 1965.

Latham J.B. — *THE LOCOMOTIVES OF CROYDON GAS AND ELECTRICITY WORKS*, J.B.Latham, 1970.

Learmonth, Bob; Nash, Joanna and Cluett, Douglas (Ed) — *THE FIRST CROYDON AIRPORT, 1915-1928*, Sutton Libraries and Arts Services 1977.

Living History Publications — *RETRACING CANALS TO CROYDON AND CAMBERWELL*, Living History Publications, 1986.

Misson, R.J. — *A HISTORICAL SURVEY OF THE OMNIBUS ROUTES AND SERVICES WITHIN THE LONDON BOROUGH OF CROYDON AREA, SUMMER 1995*, Manuscript in Croydon Local Studies Library.

Mitchell, Vic and Smith, Keith — *CATERHAM AND TATTENHAM CORNER*, Middleton Press, 1993.

Mitchell, Vic and Smith, Keith — *CROYDON (WOODSIDE) TO EAST GRINSTEAD,.* Middleton Press, 1995.

Mitchell, Vic and Smith, Keith — *EAST CROYDON TO THREE BRIDGES*, Middleton Press, 1988.

Mitchell, Vic and Smith, Keith — *LONDON BRIDGE TO EAST CROYDON*, Middleton Press, 1988.

Mitchell, Vic and Smith, Keith — *MITCHAM JUNCTION LINES*, Middleton Press, 1992.

Mitchell, Vic and Smith, Keith — *VICTORIA TO EAST CROYDON*, Middleton Press, 1987.

Mitchell, Vic and Smith, Keith — *WEST CROYDON TO EPSOM*, Middleton Press, 1992.

Robbins, George — *TILLING IN LONDON*, Capital Transport, 1986.

Russell, Terry — *CROYDON'S TROLLEYBUSES*, Middleton Press, 1996.

Skinner, M.W.G. — *CROYDON'S RAILWAYS*, Kingfisher Railway Productions, 1985.

Spence, Jeoffrey. — *THE CATERHAM RAILWAY, REVISED EDITION*, The Oakwood Press, 1986.

Stearn, Bob. — *CROYDON CARS*, Stearn Publishing, Croydon 1985.

Stewart, Michael; Gent, John and Stannard, Colin. — *TRAMLINK HANDBOOK*, Capital Transport, 2000.

Turner, J.T.Howard. — *THE LONDON, BRIGHTON & SOUTH COAST RAILWAY*
I) *ORIGINS AND FORMATION* Batsford, 1977.
II) *ESTABLISHMENT AND GROWTH* Batsford, 1978
III) *COMPLETION AND MATURITY* Batsford, 1979.

Local directories published by Gray, Warren and Ward from 1851 onwards and local newspapers from 1855 are invaluable sources of information. The Local Studies Library in Katharine Street holds a vast stock of illustrations, publications and records for reference purposes.

Acknowledgements

The illustrations in this publication are from the following sources and are reproduced by their kind permission. In some cases it has not been possible to trace the photographer or holder of the copyright, but their contribution is nevertheless gratefully acknowledged.

Harold Bennett — Nos 177 and 178.
David Bradley — Nos 180 and 181.
Terry Cooper — No 78.
A.B. Cross — No 142.
B.J. Cross — Nos 187,188,190,193,194,195,196 and 200.
B.J. Cross Collection — No 160.
Colour-Rail — Nos 60,61,62,69,70,71,72 and 73.
Chorley Handford — Nos 84 and 132.
Croydon Advertiser — Nos 117 and 120.
Croydon Airport Society — Nos 216,217 and 221.
Croydon Local Studies Library — Frontispiece and numbers 4,5,6,7,8,10,14,17,19,21,22,24,25,26,28,32,33,36,37,38,39,41,45,49,54,55,58,65,86,92,93,94,99,100,106,109,111,112,114,122,124,128,130,136,163,164,191,203,206 and back cover.
Croydon Museum and Heritage Service — Nos 9,13 and 30.
Graham Donaldson — Nos 79,80,81,82,143,146,147,149,150,197 and 198.

John Gent — Front Cover and Numbers 23,83,116,119,144,145,148,192,199 and 220.
John Gent Collection — Nos 1,2,3,11,12,15,16,20,27,29,34,40,42,43,44,46,47,48,50,52,53,56,63,85,88,89,90,91,95,96,97,101,102,103,104,105,110,113,118,121,123,125,127,129,131,137,139,152,153,154,155,156,157,158,159,161,162,165,166,167,169,170,171,172,173,174,175,182,184,185,189,202,204,205,207,208,209,210,211,212,213,214,215,218 and 219.
Walter Gratwicke — No 168.
Tim Harding — Nos 98,107 and 108.
Mike Harris — No 186.
D.W.K. Jones — No 140.
John Meredith — Nos 64,66,67,68,74,75,87 and 183.
Ray Misson — No 126.
Tony Moss — No 141.
Omnibus Society — No 138.
A.D.Packer — No 176.
Stuart Pickford — No 115.
John Price — No 77.
R.C.Riley Collection — Nos 51,57,59,76 and 133.
Terry Russell — No 179.
Brian Salter — No 18.
Peter Walker — Nos 31,35,134,135,151 and 201.

The Editor and Council of CNHSS also wish to record their appreciation of the help given by the following in this production; Steve Roud and the staff of Croydon Local Studies Library, Dave Smith (Memories of Hendon), Terry Cooper, Graham Donaldson, Mike Hutchins, Tim Harding, Ken Glazier, John Meredith and John Minnis. Also particular thanks to Peter Walker for producing some splendid maps.

Old Photographs, Postcards, Maps, Documents and other items of local interest

Croydon Local Studies Library, or the Society would appreciate the donation or loan of items of local interest. Anyone able to assist is requested to write to the Local Studies Librarian or the Secretary of CNHSS.

CNHSS

The Croydon Natural History and Scientific Society

THE SOCIETY'S EMBLEM (left) Based on a bronze open-work disc found in 1893 in a Saxon cemetery in Edridge Road between Croydon High Street and Park Lane. It is a rare example of a 5th or 6th century girdle ornament or amulet and now forms part of the Croydon Clocktower collection.

By 1870, the population of Croydon had reached 50,000 and in March that year, a group of local professional men met to establish **The Croydon Microscopical Club**. The inaugural meeting was held on 6 April 1870 at the Public Halls in George Street, which was to be the Society's home for many years. The initial 80 members included most of the local doctors and many prominent townspeople.

The club soon widened its activities to include photography and other interests, changing its name to **The Croydon Microscopical and Natural History Club** in 1877 and to its present title in 1902. By this time the Society was actively campaigning for a museum in the town.

In 1912, Christopher Fagg initiated the Regional Survey of Croydon and District, widely copied in the 1920s and 1930s with a strong influence on the teaching of geography and some influence in town planning concepts.

The Croydon Natural History and Scientific Society survived two world wars and has maintained publication of its Journal (Proceedings and Transactions of CNHSS) from 1871 to the present.

In 1975 the Society was instrumental in establishing **The Croydon Society** to deal with general town planning and conservation issues.

In 1971 Walter Bennett, a member since 1923, died and left his collections to CNHSS forming the basis of the Society's museum of archaeological, geological, local history and ethnographical artefacts, some of which form part of the collections of Croydon Clocktower. The Society's collections are available for inspection and research by arrangement with the curator.

CNHSS also maintain an extensive reference library for study purposes and with a few exceptions books are available to members on loan.

The Society organises occasional exhibitions and displays at a variety of events. There are opportunities for members to involve themselves in a number of ways or simply to learn more about the natural and local history of Croydon and beyond.

CNHSS is the longest established local voluntary organisation in Croydon

- has published Proceedings since 1871

- was involved in establishing Croydon Camera club in 1890

- helped set up the Photographic Survey & Record of Surrey in 1902

- helped to save Croham Hurst from redevelopment

- helped to save the Whitgift Hospital from demolition

- established the Regional Survey of Croydon and District in 1912

- was involved in setting up Croydon Astronomical Society

- initiated the Croydon Society in 1975

- has published eight illustrated local history books since 1970

- arranges around 80 meetings and visits each year

- has around 450 members

- has consistently campaigned for a Croydon museum

- is a company limited by guaranteed without share capital

- is a registered charity recognised by Croydon Education Authority

- is an educational body

- has a national reputation

- was awarded a Millennium Lottery Grant to establish a 'Museum without walls' Heritage Trail at stops on the new Croydon Tramlink system

---

The Society has eight sections, each of which arranges its own programme.

ARCHAEOLOGY Occasional assistance is given with professional archaeological digs. Lectures are held on local and national topics with visits to sites of special interest.

BOTANY Regular lectures and field meetings including recording schemes and conservation projects. The Croydon area has some interesting botanical rarities.

ENTOMOLOGY Regular members' evenings are held and individual member's fieldwork is contributing to the study of insect distribution in Surrey.

GEOLOGY Regular lectures and visits on a wide range of geological interests of South East England and further afield.

Members of the Society are entitled to attend the meetings of all sections.

INDUSTRIAL STUDIES Croydon and the south east is rich in sites of industrial archaeological and transport interest. Lectures and visits are arranged, throughout the year.

LOCAL HISTORY The Croydon area has a varied and interesting history. Lectures and walks are arranged and assistance given with research for the Society's publications.

METEOROLOGY Occasional meetings are held which continue the society's pioneering studies of local weather during the 19th Century.

ORNITHOLOGY Lectures and field meetings covering sites and topics of ornithological interest in Croydon, the south east generally and worldwide.

CNHSS OBJECTIVES:

To encourage the study of the sciences especially the natural and local history and archaeology of the Croydon area by organising lectures, members talks, discussions, exhibitions, outdoor meetings, visits and surveys, by issuing publications and by maintaining a library and a museum.

The Society is concerned with original investigation, conservation, curation, education and incidental recreation.

WHY NOT JOIN NOW AND HELP US IN OUR LOCAL EFFORTS?

WE WELCOME NEW MEMBERS

Croydon Natural History & Scientific Society
96A Brighton Road
South Croydon
Surrey CR2 6AD